# HOW TO

# GET RICH

# SLOW

## *BE SUCCESSFUL BY FINDING*

## *WINDOWS OF OPPORTUNITY*

## Franklin Weeks

Lovstad Publishing
Poynette, Wisconsin
Lovstadpublishing@live.com

ISBN: 0615762506
ISBN-13: 978-0615762500

Printed in the United States of America

Cover design by Lovstad Publishing

# CONTENTS

# HOW TO

# GET RICH

# SLOW

# FOREWORD

*"Progress, of the best kind, is comparatively slow. Great results cannot be achieved at once; and we must be satisfied to advance in life as we walk, step by step."*
~ Samuel Smiles (Scottish Author, 1812 – 1904)

Every individual stands on the precipice of life with a world of opportunity ahead.

What will the future bring? What kind of life do you envision for yourself? As you read the book I suggest you think a bit about what is best for you. If you force yourself to have the discipline and work hard you can be very successful in your own business without taking great risks or because you were a born genius.

Many people find a good job with a big corporation. They build a pension and buy a home and pay for it. They live a pretty good life, and if conservative, they can educate their children, be active in the community and be respected. They can have hobbies, take trips and have little to worry about at the job. The savings and the pension give the security and the ability to travel or be involved in things they like to do. Is that so bad? No, not really.

It does not give you airplanes to go anywhere and whenever you want. It does not give you money to do good things as you grow old. Should you make a plan to build a large successful business you will have days of unexpected problems. A truck may have an accident and kill someone. Employees may be hurt. You may justly or unjustly be sued and ruin a year waiting for trial.

Maybe you wish you could do some of the things suggested, and maybe you just want to make your retirement more pleasant.

Do believe you can do it if you choose and apply yourself. But the success comes with some tradeoffs. We are victims of habit and if you build the organization it will be hard to stop. We know of successful people buying companies into their 90s.

Think it over.

*If you are sure you can do it or if you are sure you cannot do it, you are right.* HENRY FORD


I have had a career with business success and a good life. I have created net worth, good friends, good health and good family and have had many good times. My career started with a gas station business when I was 18 and later built a modular home business that is one of the largest in the Midwest market to this day. We have radio stations; we manufacture commercial parabolic antennas, tracking systems for solar electricity, apartments, land development, farming and a mortgage company. I have been a bank director for many years.

Most business ventures are okay. Some are great. Some of my best investments were good businesses that were not unique. This book is about regular good business opportunities but also about finding and taking advantage of some special "windows of opportunity".

Is it difficult to become a multimillionaire? No.

Do you have to be the smartest kid in the class? No.

Do you have to risk it all to be successful? Not at all.

You can read about people who failed five times and then became a success. Being a success is not worth the grief of one failure. You do not need to take big gambles.

What is the easiest way to be worth $3,000,000.00 at retirement? You and your significant other start smoking cigarettes. Good ones, the expensive kind. Then quit. Save the almost $8 a pack and invest in one of the big low fee index funds that should yield 7% over the long term. Upon retirement, if you really do this, you would have in 52 years $2,754,064.00 (this would work for a nonsmoker, too) If cigarette prices go up, increase the investment, knowing inflation is here and you will have a lot more money but you cannot buy any more stuff.

Smoking causes cancer, heart failure and impotence; all probably hurt.

Frank Weeks, 2012

## My personal history

I was the third child. I was born in the depth of the depression. My father who was 25 years old worked for the WPA. My father passed away from pneumonia the week I was born. My mother, with the help of parents raised the three children. She remarried in 1941. They had another child and we all lived on a Wisconsin farm.

During the 1940s our farm had no electricity. The Rural Cooperatives had wired most of the country but had not come to our farm yet. We farmed with horses as we did not have a tractor. There was, of course, no running water and the water was supplied by a windmill. The heat was from wood stoves. Information and entertainment was from a battery powered radio. Education beyond High school would be difficult without money.

My life goal was to run a gas station as I loved cars and thought I was a fair mechanic. After high school I worked in a gas station. Probably because of the good farm work ethic, the owner asked if I would like to run a gas station of my own and be in business. I said yes and with $100 of savings to put in the cash register, I was in business leasing and operating a gas station.

My friends with good jobs made $2000 a year by working 40 hours a week for $1.00 an hour. I was able to earn $3000 a year because I was in business and worked 60 hours a week. I enjoyed it and I was always trying to be a good person. I could hardly say no to someone who wanted credit and was not aggressive in trying to get the money owed to me. I was learning. I had bought a mediocre business with marginal profits. I had bought a bad job.

In 1954 La Crosse, Wisconsin was getting a TV station. There was no TV in rural America but big cities like Chicago had TV during the 1940s. I wanted a TV. I had bought few things new in my life and so I wanted a used TV. I knew that used ones would be available in Chicago; I asked my friend to go with me to Chicago to buy a TV set and I found a "window of opportunity."

Arriving in Chicago I asked someone where could I buy a used TV and they said "Polk Brothers is the largest chain of stores in Chicago and they take trade ins and they have a used TV store on Grand Avenue." I went to Polk Brothers and bought as many TV sets as I could put into my Oldsmobile. I sold them all quickly at a big profit. I recognized a window of opportunity with high margins and so I sold the gas stations and began selling used TV sets to dealers in locations that were getting new TV stations.

While making a living selling used TV sets I also bought a building lot and started building a house. I thought I was a good builder (I was not) and I designed the house myself as I was sure I was a good designer. (I was not) I put up the house with a too big living room, too small bedrooms, too much hall, and I hurried with my work as I did not have patience.

I also learned something about how good people are. If you ask for help people are usually willing. You may think that if you ask a plumber how to vent a bathroom he would not help you as he would feel you are taking work away from him. Not so, especially if you are young. I found I could ask an electrician how to wire something and he would be very helpful. *Good people* like to be helpful.

The house was strong but lacking excellent workman-ship.

In 1959 I was drafted into the army with an unfinished house. When you build a house it includes a foundation, framing, and shingling, plumbing, heating, wiring, drywall, insulation, cabinets and trim. If a house is worth $10,000 as they often were in 1959, if you do everything yoursellf it costs much less. If you hire nothing it would cost about $4000. I was going into the Army so I sold my home and put the money in a bank drawing interest. I got married on the leave after basic training and spent two years in the army as a clerk.

I could type fast and so while trained to be in the con-struction engineers I was put into a battalion office. My job soon became simple and I could do it well in 2 hours a day. I had 6 hours to spend doing something else. The military had wonderful manuals on everything and one of my jobs was to requisition needed manuals. I found I could learn anything I wanted by spending the 6 hours a day reading manuals.

I had always had an interest in electronics as I had ex-posure to the functions and was able to repair simple things on TV sets. At that time there were no transistors or integrated circuits used but the function of the circuits was the same. Electricity had to be amplified, oscillated to ob-tain needed frequency's, mixed together and detected, and power supplies need to be created to take the AC and make it usable DC by being transformed, rectified and filtered to make it usable. I developed a basic understanding and had a good education except that self-training leaves you knowing a lot about many things but missing others. The good news: I was learning many things about many things.

Leaving the Army two years later I had a wife and child and wanted employment. I found a job and my first goal was to build another house. I built it, and then another, and I was renting them out. I did all the work to build them. I did the carpentry, drywall, plumbing, heating, wiring, floor covering and the cabinets.

My friends were all great people but they had newer cars and made payments on depreciating assets. When you have a great net worth you can buy silly, fun things (boats, airplanes, trips) and it does not matter. When you are starting to build a net worth and a future this should be avoided. Wait for "some day."

House number three was a better plan because I copied a plan of a good selling home and changed it just a bit to suit me. Lesson learned. Copy something good and try to improve it. I will never be in the boat building business. If I were, I would look at all the boats of the successful boat builders and if the 30' boat was a great seller I would make it nicer and 32' long and sell it as a great value.

I looked at the current market for homes and noticed that mobile homes were being built flashy and cheap and sold well. The laws were changed mostly for that industry. It was possible to build things and transport them up to 16' wide.

It occurred to me that a home could be built to state building codes and great savings could be made by buying in quantity, building inside a building and bringing complete modules on site for finished homes. I had found another window of opportunity. In May of 1966 I started our company that today is a leader in building new homes in the Midwest

As our companies grew I did many other things that were worthwhile and fun to do. Some were better than others. A lesson also learned is: always be looking at things and seeing how it is made and could you make it better. Curiosity is a wonderful trait. Owning and operating apartments is a great business that gives a good return and shelters net worth from inflation. Radio stations are a good business. Our mortgage company is a good business. Our retail of building materials store is a good business taking advantage of our big house materials inventory. While good, they are not unique opportunities.

Always be looking because you might find a wonderful "Window of opportunity."

My Windows of opportunity were:

Ace TV

Building homes doing 100 % of everything

Building modular homes

Dh satellite

Dh solar

I was raised on a farm and loved the open areas. After I had my house building company going well, I looked for a farm to live on. I found a farm of 160 acres with the back side on a river. I sold 50 acres and the buildings. I put in a long driveway and built our home. This farm home is just 8 minutes from my office and an ideal place to live and raise a family.

When my children were young we were part time farmers and enjoyed raising cattle, planting corn and putting up hay. As time went on and the children grew up, we decided to rent out the land.

This is a great farm and what is interesting is that land rent gives income that will pay the taxes and insurance. The farm has a solar panel tracker to make electricity so it has no electrical bills. With a private well there is no water or sewer bill. I have often wondered why people choose to live in a city when they could live better and for less in the country.

As I became older I chose to spend much of my time in a warmer climate. With the internet you can live anyplace and keep excellent contact with your business interests and people.

I am fortunate that I have a great family. Many things in life are the result of your efforts. Regarding your children and their choice of partners in life you need also to be lucky. I have been lucky and so I am officially retired. As I am a senior citizen I know that in the future I will be gone. My life's work of building business interests is still important to me and I want it to continue after I am gone. By being available for advice while away is good. Letting them make decisions gives my heirs the experience of running our companies without me. I am pleased that many things in our business interests run better without my day to day decisions.

Picasso was quoted as saying: *If it is good copy it, and if it is a great idea, steal it!*

## ACE TV: My first big
## Window of Opportunity

In the 1950's TV sets were expensive and not very good. They were hand built with each component soldered in place. As there were no transistors everything was tubes. The tubes had a short life and every town had people who fixed tube radios and then TV sets. As the early TV stations were put up just before or after WW2 the big cities were the only TV markets. Each big city would get a station or two and TV sets were made usually in that city. During the 1950s TV stations were being built in smaller cities and the market for TV sets was growing. The price of a new TV was expensive. Usually around $400 when an average worker was making about $1 an hour or $2,000 a year.

I was successfully running my gas station in 1954 when a new TV station was being built in La Crosse Wisconsin. TV came on only in the evening and went off the air about midnight. The programs were mostly recorded as it was difficult to get signals to the stations. Coaxial cables were being run to bring signals to cities and some microwave towers were being put up.

I wanted a TV set. I was aware that Chicago had many TV stations and that used TV sets were available.

They had hundreds of used TV sets. They would check each one out and put a number on the picture tube. A TV with a number one had been tested and worked well. Number thirty one indicated the picture tube was broken. Each other number was telling what was wrong with it.

Two worked but rolled vertically. Three had no sound, four the picture tipped over etc.

Some TV sets were in really big cases but with a small picture tube, like six inches. Some were with long wired remote controls. A Muntz brand has nine tubes and worked. It worked poorly when far from the TV station. A RCA TV had about thirty tubes and was much better. All TV sets had a notation on the back that they were built to the patents owned by RCA. I bought six TV sets that worked and brought them back to my gas station. I hooked them all up and put a price on them.

I paid $1 an inch so a six inch cost me $6 and a seventeen inch cost $17. I put a price with a big markup on each one and sold them all in a few days.

I borrowed a pickup truck and went back to Chicago and bought ten sets and the next week sold them with a big markup. Soon I was making much more money on the TV sets then the gas station. It was fun and I went back to Chicago and bought more and more.

One of the gas station customers wanted to buy the gas station and so I sold it.

I was in the used TV business. I bought a used 1 ½ ton truck and painted it red. I lettered the side ACE TV and went to Chicago. I could put 50 TV sets in the truck and I put cardboard between each one. I would buy a case of Old English polish to make them look good.

I would usually drive to Chicago on Monday and stay overnight. I would buy 50 TV sets and head west. I knew that Mason City had a new station on the air so by late Tuesday I was selling the TV sets wholesale to TV repair shops with a $10 markup each. I would sell them all by

Wednesday and come back home to spend money the rest of the week.

When I would buy 50 TV sets that worked the man selling them would give me some that did not work. I learned how to fix many of them.

I was a kid. I did not really become aggressive in taking advantage of the short time window of opportunity. I was usually back by Thursday for a long weekend. I tried hard to spend the money on fun and of course included a boat for real fun times.

I would take a week off often and then go back and buy 50 sets and go a different direction to sell them. It got cold so I went to Arizona to see an Aunt and stayed for a month.

I did OK financially but did not really take advantage of my opportunity. If I would have worked a 6 day week and drove a truck selling and taking orders for more I could have made not only big profits, but I could have built a permanent business. I could have started a retail store and had employees doing the pickup and delivery. In just a few years this business was not going to exist. The costs of new TV sets went down and soon there were used trade in TV sets available in every market. I did drive around the Midwest calling on TV repair shops and selling sets. I became a better sales person. Each TV station was a different frequency so an ideal antenna could have been made for that station. I could easily have manufactured and sold antennas and the cable and other supplies.

If I had been mature, made brochures, had a phone number so they could call when they wanted more I could have had a business that could grow and soon maybe be a distributor of new TV sets. If I were more mature I could have started a chain of stores selling electronics.

I did not take advantage of the big window of opportunity because I was young and maybe a bit lazy or not motivated.

I learned that some businesses were better than others. In spite of my youth I did create a net worth that allowed me to build my first house. I was a silly kid that was successful in spite of all the things I did wrong.

When I was selling used TV sets I sold many with the brand name Muntz. I also was also very interested in cars and was aware of a sports car that was a Muntz brand. I also was aware that in the 1960s and 1970s the big boom in HiFi equipment with ads that featured Mad Man Muntz. This was a California based company. In the mid 1980s I attended many satellite shows and I was in California in our booth selling antennas. An older gentleman came into the booth with a name tag of Muntz. I asked if he was related to the Muntz TV and he said yes he started the company. I then asked about the Muntz sports car and he said that was him. He explained that he left the Chicago area and moved to California to develop the HiFi music equipment business. He said he was fascinated with Satellite TV so he attended the show but said he had cancer and was not going to be long for the world. What a neat guy with a great career. I recently saw a TV collector car auction with a Muntz sport car from 1950 sell for more than $100,000.00

## Building My First Home

As I have mentioned I thought I was a good designer so I designed my own new home. I made a strong home but with a bad design. I had an uncle that was building homes and renting them out and so I would often go and help him and he agreed when I built a home he would also help me.

My first home did not have a basement. In Wisconsin a new homes needs a foundation under the frost. I put in a footing of concrete and laid cements blocks. As you need to go down 4' for the foundation going another 4' and putting in a basement is not expensive. Instead I had a crawl space. This was a mistake in a Wisconsin home.

Room sizes were wrong and the layout was wrong but it was a house. I did all the work. I did hire a plumbing contractor to bring the water and sewer into the house but I did everything else.

I added a nice garage and built it with funds I had. I would not have enough to buy some things I needed so I did inexpensive things. I picked rocks from a creek and laid up a rock wall on part of the front of the home.

A lesson is that going ahead doing something you know little about is better than not doing anything. I made my own roof trusses. I had my uncle help put them on the house. I put on boards for floor sheathing, roof sheathing and wall sheathing. Installed the insulation, the drywall and roughed in the electrical wiring and plumbing. I had the windows in place and the exterior walls in place. I rolled texture on the drywall and soon had a pretty good looking unfinished house.

What did I do right? I built a house. What did I do wrong? Almost everything else. I should have looked at new homes for sale and realized that I had a bad plan and could take an existing plan, try to improve it and have a better house. I was a moderately sensible person. I was single and not very motivated. I knew I had military service ahead.

Today with a company that has built many thousands of new homes in 50 years I realize what I like means little. What other people like is important. As we go into a new year we review what people have purchased from us. We look at the options they like. They are the buyers and what they like is important and what I like is not important.

I knew I was going to be drafted into the army.

I knew I had found the girl I would marry.

Plans are hard to make when you are waiting for the call. Each month people would volunteer and so your draft number would move back but I finally got the call to serve. I listed the house as an unfinished home and it sold quickly. I put the money in the bank and went off to the Army to return a more mature person.

## The home builder: My second big
## Window of Opportunity

It was 1961and I was let out of the Army. I found a job. I worked from noon until 9 in the evening at my job and spent my mornings building a new home. Again with little experience I thought I should be the designer so I built another house that was better than the first one but also poorly designed.

While in the military we purchased a used trailer to live in. We made a down payment and financed it to be paid in full in 18 months. We were conservative and actually saved money while in the Army. I recall I was paid in cash $82 a month and my wife received $137.10 a month.

We lived in the trailer while building my first home and completed it the first summer and moved in. The house was about 900 sq feet. It included us doing everything. I built the cabinets and had to do many things twice as I was learning. Because I did everything, this modest home was paid for from the savings from the first home. We then had another baby. I had developed a good habit of working hard and being productive.

We decided to build another house and rent the first one out. I sold the trailer and started a second home with the funds. So in 1962 I spent my mornings building a house. We did not have enough money so we borrowed some money to complete it. I recall I financed it for two years. I rented the first house and with my paycheck and rent paid the loan in less than two years. The second home had a much better floor plan and improved workmanship.

While the first one was strong it did not have excellent workmanship.

My banker was a lady who complimented me on my success. It was so comforting to be able to show her a balance sheet that showed the value of the house, my savings and my net worth. I developed a good relationship with my banker. At that time I was driving a used 1953 Chevy that I had bought for cash. A personal banker friend is comforting. I found that with my being willing to work 12 hours days and get paid for 8 hours I was building net worth. I was able to build new homes that were worth much more than cost.

I made the foundation by pouring a concrete footing. I used cement blocks to lay up the basement walls. I mixed the concrete from the sand on the site, buying bags of cement. I did all the carpentry, putting on floor joists, floor boards (not plywood—old carpenters said it was better and I believed them). Framing the walls and raising them up. I had noticed that carpenters would cut a wall stud and write pattern on it and mark the rest before they cut them. I instead marked one, cut one and continued. Each stud grew in height the width of my pencil mark. When I raised the last wall I was a half inch higher than the first. I had to take them down and re cut them. I was learning.

I made the roof framing, and sheathed everything. I put on shingles. I put on siding. I bought windows that were not assembled and was working hard and learning. The houses were not perfect but they were strong. I would put in hardwood flooring and sand it and finish it. The plumbing would require a master plumber if you were doing it for someone else but I would do it myself. I learned to pour lead joints on the cast iron pipe. I learned how to sweat the copper tubing water lines. I understood electricity and did all of my wiring.

As I finished my third house and started my fourth I could create a balance sheet that showed the value of my homes, my personal property and money in the bank and show my very little debt. I could see I was building a considerable net worth—a net worth along with good credit that would allow me to do many things in the future.

When general contractors build a home, they hire help, have overhead, and want to make a profit. They hire people who may or may not be real efficient. By doing everything you do not save half, you save at least 60 percent of the value. You are making money that you are not taxed on until and if you sell it. At that time it is taxed at a lower capital gain rate. Most people do not want to work 12 hours a day and every weekend. Today with the requirement of engineered plans, fees for inspectors, rules for license for each trade it would be very difficult to do. But for me it built a net worth that could allow me to do many other things.

## Modular homes: My third big Window of Opportunity

Because of my personal building experience my employer suggested a new business he would own. We would be a general contractor building new homes. I agreed. I would manage it, sell the homes and run the company.

I would quote a price for a new home that included subcontractors doing the work. I would hire an excavation contractor to dig the basement and later back fill and grade the property. A basement contractor that would pour the footings, walls and basement floor, a plumbing contractor, an electrical contractor, a carpenter crew to frame and finish the home, drywall people, floor covering contractor, cabinet supplier. The homes would be quoted with known bids and materials quotations. I would add an IF factor (my ignorance factor), then add profit and sell the home. During the next few years I contracted for more than 100 new homes. I continued to build homes for myself in my spare time.

During and after the Second World War many trailers were built. The width allowed was 8 feet so they were typically 8' x 30' and temporary housing. During the 1950s and 1960s laws were changed that allowed them to be wider and so 10' wide x 50' long became popular. Then 12' wide and 14' wide up to 70' long were being built and many bought them as their permanent housing. During the 1970s they became about 25% of all new homes in the country. Dealers and manufacturers wanted to get away from the trailer image and so they changed the name to

Mobile homes. As many were built cheaply or were placed in very poor mobile home parks the image still was not good so it was then changed to Manufactured homes. These were and are under the control of federal standards but were sold mostly because of low prices. They were and still are with steel frames and can be relocated. As many trailers were really bad the federal government created the standards for their construction.

State laws were enacted creating building codes for homes built on site. Homes were improving in quality and safety.

Two things were happening in the US. Plywood was becoming the good building material product. The homes I had built used lumber but plywood was stronger and if you glued it to the lumber framing before it was nailed it became much stronger and big plywood beams were being built. It was called a stress skinned beam. The laws in the Midwest were allowing movement to be up to16 feet wide. I had my epiphany. Why not build a house exactly like the homes I was building on site and wrap them in plywood that was glued. This would make them strong enough to move without a built in steel frame.

I thought I could make a house to the state building codes that would allow me to build them in a factory in two or more pieces. We would use a temporary frame to move them to a foundation and assemble them in modules and have a home that had many advantages. It never got wet as it was built inside a building and the expensive things, like plumbing, heating, wiring, floor covering and cabinets could be done without contractors.

In May of 1966 I talked my employer into investing

with me to form a new corporation. I put some of my personal rental homes on the market, sold them for my share of the investment and we formed the corporation. It was agreed I would run it, he would be an investor. We built a factory building that was 80 feet wide and 180 feet long and started business.

In the fall of 1966 we built six new homes. While a tax loss on paper I could show the bankers that we really had a profit valuing things at more than depreciation showed. It worked well and we continued in 1967 and built 44 new homes. Again a paper loss but an increase in real value of assets. In 1968 we built 108 new homes and were a very profitable business and paying taxes. In November of 1968 a fork lift in the factory broke a gasoline line and the operator turned it off. It leaked gas on the exhaust and the building started on fire. 4 homes were lost but everyone got out OK. It was a crisis. My banker came to see me and said they were there to help and not to worry. Good banking relationships are wonderful.

I rented a temporary facility and made it through the winter into 1969 and another good year.

We were on our way. We rebuilt the factory and expanded it.

This type of home became known as modular homes and while manufactured, they were not technically manufactured homes.

My partner chose to sell his interest to me and the company continued to grow.

We have never shut down or stopped production except for holidays or inventory. We are now a company more than 46 years old and the largest builder of our type of home sold direct in our market. We have 20 sales locations that cover the nine states we sell in. We have sales locations near Kansas City, Lincoln Nebraska, all over Wisconsin, Minnesota and have built many thousands of new homes.

We borrowed money to build the factory. We borrowed more money to expand; we borrowed more money because it made sense to have an inventory built in the winter to sell in the summer to those that were in a hurry. We borrowed money to buy three radio stations and build subdivisions and build sales locations. Our goal, though, was to get out of debt. The debt was of two types. Seasonal borrowing and long term debt on buildings. We paid off all long term debt in 1985 and made it through the season of 1990 without short term borrowing. We have not borrowed money since.

During the years of 1967 through 1972 I was too modest to make the claim but I really thought I was pretty smart. I did OK but I was lucky. The market fluctuates and the mid-west is primarily agricultural states. Those were good years for farmers. I found that all years were not good years and that to be building equity was important.

Now years later our modular homes are built to the same codes as on site except better. Not a bit better but way, way, way better. They are never rained on during construction. Because we could work inside with perfect weather, as we could purchase in greater quantities for lower prices we created the best value. We know our new homes are the best value. Most people living in a 30 year old modular home we built do not know the home was built in pieces. Most people borrow money for a new home so they need an appraisal. We use 7-ply real Douglas fir plywood in the floors while most use a OSB. Our homes have more insulation with R-50 in the ceiling, the best plumbing, *KOHLER*, the best heating system, *LENNOX*, the best of everything but cost less. Our homes when completed are worth more than they cost according to the appraisal.

One time while visiting with a person I mentioned we had built the home they lived in. They said we had not as their home was a brick home. I said we designed the foundation with a brick ledge and had it bricked when it was done. They loved the home.

My Design Home on a bluff overlooking the
Mississippi River in Marquette Iowa

Typical Design homes

## Selling Homes Factory Direct

I sold homes direct from the factory from a display of two homes. I also sold them "wholesale" to dealers who had to pay for delivery and complete them. Other people started to build modular homes and soon we had many competitors. We continued to sell most of them direct but many at wholesale to dealers. Building and selling to dealers was easy. Take the order, build them and then it was up to the dealers. Most of the early dealers were also mobile home dealers and not all were doing a good job. As we continued I found that selling direct was much more difficult. I needed to buy expensive cranes to set them on basements. I needed to have crews to go on site and finish them and to service any problems.

Something else became evident. All my new competitors were selling all homes to dealers. Also I found most of my service problems were not from homes we sold but homes dealers sold and did not finish properly or made promises that were wrong. Our direct sales could be less money for the ultimate user and more profitable for us. There were fewer problems caused by the dealer who often could or would not pay as agreed. Our policy changed and we became all factory direct. One advantage of factory direct is we could build it better. Talking to a home prospect and telling them we want to use the good *Kohler* toilet and it does cost just a little more and they agree. A dealer would say, "no, put in the cheapest you can find so I can make more money." Customers preferred to buy direct and today, years later our company has 20 sales locations from Kansas City, Missouri to Northern Minnesota. Our record of production in our best year was 14 new homes a week and 700 new homes built in one year.

## Mortgage Company

Most new homes are built on site by contractors. Most people need a loan to buy a home so an appraisal is done. Most lenders want 20% down and a history of good credit and income to qualify. In the big cities most homes are in subdivisions owned and controlled by the builder and he wants to build a home you choose after looking at the models. In rural areas the local contractor agrees to build a plan chosen by the customer and usually the local bank will make the loan.

The customer applies to the bank and supplies the plan and the estimates from the usual subcontractors that include the basement, the plumber, the electrician, the carpenter, the drywall contractor, the floor covering people and the lumber supplier. They often have guaranteed fixed bids so the project gets approved by the bank and begins. As it progresses the contractors try to upgrade everything and so the costs have overruns. Usually this is not a problem as the banker knew that it would happen.

I have been a bank director and have been on loan committees for many years. If the loan is high enough that it is brought to the loan committee we review and discuss it. Always, the loan officer will explain that he has anticipated some overruns. The cost is maybe $250,000 and the loan is maybe $200,000 and the home owner is excellent and has $50,000 down payment so it is a good loan. When the project is done and the cost is $275,000 and the loan is really $225,000 it is still an OK loan.

When we began, the banks would anticipate big overruns and would figure them in. Banks love good real estate loans but worry about construction loans. We had people turned down by the bank for this fear and instead they would encourage them to buy an existing home.

We saw a window of opportunity as we knew exactly what the costs were to be and there were no overruns. We started a Mortgage company. We did construction loans and also loans that could be resold as securities. This became an excellent business as it created sales for us and is a profit center.

As time went on we often found people that needed financing for shorter times and it was possible for us to keep the loan and profit by the interest we charged. Even for a loan that is made for construction and then sold to a pool of loans there is a fee that generates income.

Creating a mortgage company was starting a business that is profitable and also is able to help the main business.

## Garage Business

We sold homes for many years and they did not include a garage. Our feeling was that a garage did not have plumbing, heating, much wiring, any cabinets and floor covering and we probably could not create a better value traveling and building the garage on site.

Many people said, "I can help my brother-in-law build the garage and he will work for beer." I felt we did not need to build garages.

But, a problem arose. Someone would plan to buy a new custom home from us and would then go to the local builder and ask for a garage quote. The builder would say, "Let me build the whole project as I can be competitive." The result was a lost sale for us and a longer wait and problems with cost over runs for the buyer.

A garage attached is usually three exterior walls, roof trusses, plywood and shingles, overhead and walk in doors. We decided to create a garage crew. We prebuilt the walls and the trusses and purchased a light truck mounted crane. We put a hitch on this vehicle and pulled a trailer with the walls and the other materials that were needed to build a garage. The crews were good, and soon they were very efficient and could travel a long distance and still build a complete garage in a day. We put them on a bonus program and soon we were amazed at how quickly they could build a good garage on site.

Even though we did not have those big items like plumbing, much electrical, or heating to save them money on, we could be very competitive even with travel. We now have built thousands of garages and it is an excellent business. By starting the garage program we solved a problem and turned it into a profit center.

We found a good business that alone was profitable but also helped another part of the company. We still cannot compete with the brother-in-law that will build it for beer, but we sell a lot of garages.

## Satellite Antennas: My fourth big
## Window of Opportunity

In the late 1970s I was aware that satellite signals were landing on my farm and hundreds of TV channels were available. They were of a very high frequency but they were simple analogue TV signals. If I could collect them and amplify them and detect the signals in the carrier I could have free TV with hundreds of channels.

I knew that a normal antenna and amplifier would not work. I needed to collect more of the weak signal. As the frequency was 4 gigahertz. A yagi antenna like you see on roofs would have been about 1 inch across. The very, very weak signals needed to be captured and increased in strength. The size of the wave length was so small by using a reflector we could focus them onto a single spot and put the antenna there. They were still weak so they needed to be amplified without adding noise. I built a spherical reflector to concentrate these signals. I used angle iron bolted together for a frame. I drilled holes in the frame and used threaded rods and thin strips of redwood. These I adjusted to a spherical shape. I put a post in the ground 15 feet ahead of this reflector and using a wire adjusted the redwood strips. I stapled on metal window screen to reflect the signals to my feed horn. I made a large sheet metal feed horn, purchased an expensive low noise amplifier and a demodulator. Soon I had access to hundreds of channels of TV. By moving my feed horn I could receive signals from different satellites.

Satellite companies were fulfilling the Arthur C Clark

forecast in his famous paper of 1946. They were stationing satellites in orbit around the world at the equator. Arthur was most famous for his fiction but was a trained engineer. He wrote a famous paper that spoke of satellites. He was aware of the rockets that the Germans had used in the Second World War, the V1 and the V2 rockets. He calculated that with a larger rocket, a satellite could be put into orbit. He also calculated that if you put it in a low orbit it would go around the world every few hours, if

you put it in an orbit of 23,000 miles at the equator it would go around the world once a day and would appear to stand still. His paper indicated that he felt by the year 2000 there would be satellites in orbit around the equator and they would be able to transmit TV. He felt it would take that long to get fuel and an electrical generator into orbit. He did not know about solar panels and that we would have satellites in orbit years before that.

The satellite area is known as the Clark belt.

I saw a window of opportunity. I thought everyone wants to see those signals. I started a new business. I knew there would be a big interest in this. Fiberglass parabolic antennas are easy to make, are heavy, and they do work. I made a mold and had some made for me. The best receiving antennas for this high frequency, though, were a spun aluminum parabolic reflector, and so I decided to make a metal spinning lathe.

As you travel you will often see a tower with a microwave parabolic antenna. I found out they were made by spinning the aluminum against a pattern of a strong material that is a parabolic shape. While not uncommon they usually are very small and spinning machines make things like light fixtures and commercial stove hoods. I needed to hire some expert help to build really big spinning machines.

We searched for professional help. We found a company that made products from small spinning machines and with their help we built a large spinning machine. The spinning was done by a skilled worker that used tools to force the metal to the parabolic shape. This worked well and soon we experimented with more automatic machines. We used air pressure with our employee changing the pressure as the roller moved. A variable speed drive was needed to move this roller and soon we had a very automatic spinning machine. We now have a 5 meter machine that is the world's largest metal spinning machine. Today more than 30 years later DH satellite is a world leader in satellite receiver antennas For TV stations, cable companies, universities, Nexrad radar and specialty antennas sold worldwide.

Commercial parabolic antennas used by TV stations, cable companies, Nexrad radar and other commercial use.

We make antennas from 16 inches in size up to 5 meters (16 feet 4 inches). We built all the machines in house and developed equipment to do the spinning automatically.

Two tractor trailers are used to deliver them all over the US and Canada and many are shipped all over the world in containers. Some people in foreign countries buy the antennas only and paint them and build the mounts and put their private label on them. Most include the mounting systems.

Some buyers want to receive a single satellite and ask for a rigid mounting system so they can be pointed at a single satellite. Many others want it to track the arc of satellites so they can move it to access other satellites and we have a system with a linear actuator to move it. Still others want to track the complete arc. They want a full horizon to horizon system, so we install a gear box and a full chain drive system. Our top of the line system is what we call a *Gibralter* that moves separately in azimuth and in elevation. This system is very heavy duty and is preferred by engineers who want to put it on the satellite and then adjust it vertically and then horizontally so they are sure they are exactly on satellite.

We have had many requests for special antennas through the years. Many very rich people will want an antenna to receive the signals that are pointed at a far different place on the world and as this makes the signal weak at their locations they need a very large antenna. In one day we sold a large antenna to people in the Canary Islands to watch a US mainland satellite and on the same day one in Hawaii to receive the same satellite. One was looking near the horizon to the East and the other to the West.

During a period of time from 1979 when we began and 1986 when signals were scrambled, the business of 8', 10', and 12' antennas were very popular for individuals to receive free TV signals. Many companies went into the business of marketing them. Often they would buy the reflector and make other components and sell the product as their system. We had other competitors by that time making and selling antennas. One of the largest was a public company that had the parts made by others and marketed them. They bought antennas from two different sources and asked us to quote them. I thought about it for a while. They wanted the lowest possible price and wanted more people to quote.

I went to their facility and looked at what they did. I was not impressed. An employee said they load the finished product on a trailer and haul it to the fairgrounds every end of the month. I thought they were showing them as sold on the books and did not want the auditor to see they were still there. While I wanted the business I did not want them to go out of business with a big debt owed to me for the expensive aluminum. I proposed instead I would bring a spinning machine to their factory and have my employee operate it. I would do this for $25 per antenna. I felt that my only risk was the cost of the labor. A good employee could make an antenna in four minutes.

The machine was for a 10' size antenna. The machine had the mandrel (tooling shaped to a parabolic curve) and it was mounted on a large lathe we built. A flat circle of aluminum was placed on the tooling and held in place by a center piece. We put a roller against it and a motor would start to spin it. The roller was moved by an electric motor with a variable speed drive. The operator had to turn on the air and adjust it to more pressure as it moved. The control of the roller motor was to be slowed down as it moved and in three or four minutes a perfect antenna was built.

I was concerned that after a while they would build their own spinning machine and send me away. They did not really know how it worked. I asked our shop to make a muffler so when the air was taken off there was no noise. I created a useless big control panel that had digital numbers spinning up and down and had a label "digital computer control" It all worked well and became very profitable for us until they went bankrupt a few years later and only owed us a small amount for last month's labor. We took our machine back.

When the home market became big people started to make them of mesh and they worked. We started attending shows in Europe and building larger machines for commercial use. Europe and other countries chose to use a higher frequency, and so arose the need for more accurate antennas. Also I could see that there was a price war coming and the signals for home use were going to be scrambled. We realized that we needed to get into the commercial business.

We began both US and international business and were soon sending containers of antennas all over the world.

Often we get a request for a special antenna and the buyer will pay us to make the special tooling and fabricate parabolic reflectors just for them. Usually we do not know what they are for and sometimes they are used in aircraft.

The government of Taiwan wanted special antennas to receive and spy on signals from the mainland of China and we built them.

In the 1980s we sold antennas and special mounting systems to Iraq. We always required prepayment and when the Golf war of 1990 started we had a shipment that was returned to us.

A satellite will in theory stay in position in its orbit but in fact will not. The gravity of the moon and sun that causes the tides will move them. When satellites were put into orbit the plan was for a ten year life and station keeping fuel was included for ten years. The Russian satellites were the favorite satellites at that time as they were more powerful. They put many up in 1980. As they ran out of station keeping fuel they wandered. We developed an arm and special controller that would search for the satellite when the signal became lower. These were very popular during the first Gulf war in 1990.

During our 30 plus years of making satellite receiver antennas we had many competitors. Most of them were larger public companies. When digital transmission came about it became possible to add more channels by digital compression and for a while the business went into a decline. Those large public companies chose to go out of business and while the total market is smaller we are one of the last men standing, and are very busy.

## Solar Photo voltaic tracking systems:
## My fifth big Window of Opportunity

I am in Mexico reading the Wall Street Journal. I see that solar panels are becoming cheaper and that some companies instead of just pointing them south and having them work OK from 11 am to 3 pm have them follow the sun.

Eureka! I have a tracking system for tracking satellites. Satellites are at a fixed location in the sky and we make a controller so you can push a button and the parabolic antenna will go to that spot that has the desired satellite. I needed a controller that would make solar panels follow the arc of the sun and return to the east to do it every day. I needed a controller that would move it to the second. None existed. We own a golf course and use irrigation equipment. I found a high end irrigation controller that would turn on water timed to the second. I bought one and programmed it and had it switch relays. We powered a DC motor to move the solar panel to follow the sun. It worked great. We now have a commercial controller made special for this.

When the sun shines we are pointed at it and when we make more electricity than is used it makes the meter run backwards and at night it runs forward. At the end of the month if more electricity is created then used the power company must pay for it.

The arc of the sun is known. We know that we must be within 10 degrees of the sun to be efficient so our system stays within 5 degrees. Each day our controller moves the solar panels from East to west for 1 minute and 20 seconds each hour to catch the sun and pass it and stay within the 5 degrees. It stops at the horizon and at midnight moves back to the east. It does this each day. As the arc of the sun changes 2 degrees a week we have a linear arm move 8 seconds on Sunday to change this arc. The controller knows the day and so it changes direction on June 21st, the longest day, and the shortest day, December 21st.

Solar panels generate low voltage DC electricity. Our grid system is AC electricity and it is 60 cycles. As each solar cell generates a small voltage and they are connected in series to get the desired voltage. To increase the wattage these series units are connected in parallel. Today a typical solar panel will generate 200 to 300 watts. A tracking system can usually generate about 4 Kilowatts an hour. This is enough electricity for a normal home that does not waste electricity.

An important part of the system is the inverter. This is usually a heavy and expensive device that takes this DC power and changes it into AC in phase with the power company's power at 240 Volts. This connected to an electric power panel will, when the sun is shining, make the electricity you use. Should you make more then you use the meter runs backwards. During the night you do not make any so the meter runs forward. You hope the meter ends the month backwards from its start, so you make all your electricity.

Solar panels work during the hot day when the air conditioners are running. They do not work during the night when the power company does not need it. The more solar systems that exist, the less electricity needed and so the power company needs fewer power plants and less transmission lines. At this time there is a credit from the federal government for wind and solar systems. Some states also have subsidies and some power companies have promotions to encourage such installations.

Sun tracking solar panels creating electricity for a factory

*A discovery is said to be an accident meeting a prepared mind.* Anna Pavlova

Most others tracking the sun use a computer all day long searching for the sun. We choose to polar track its arc. By polar tracking our system must be installed so it is pointed exactly south (or North in the southern hemisphere) it must pivot at its latitude. It would be flat at the equator and vertical at the North Pole. The panels, though, must point at the sun so it must tip forward for the shortest days and backwards for the longest days. This is all done automatically with our system and controller.

Prototype 2 axis tracker that has supplied all of the electricity for this 3000 sq ft home for the past three years

This is a field with 21 solar tracking systems that generate more than 120,000,000 watt hours of electricity a year for a school.

Our competitors in the solar industry usually bolt the solar panels to a roof and they are fixed. By tracking we gain efficiency. Some problems exist in tracking. It is a mechanical system that needs maintenance and if you align them close together east and west they can shadow each other. We found some sites that had large trees and buildings that shadow the panels so we install a similar system that does not track the arc but rather sits pointing South. It has a simple hand crank on it so that the home owner can crank it to Summer in March and in Sept crank it to winter and it will be about 8 % more efficient than a totally fixed system.

We then found some people wanted to place them on roofs and track so we developed a weighted non roof piercing system that is manufactured mostly from galvanized pipe. It only moves to track the sun from East to West and does not make an adjustment for the changing seasons. This system is much less expensive and does not require a foundation and also is re-locatable. Because it can be installed with two modules and four solar panels it can create 1,000 watts an hour of electricity but can be ground mounted and added to. You could start with 4 modules with 8 panels and 2 kilowatts and if you generate half of your electricity you know you need a total of 8 modules and 4 kilowatts. Should you sell the property and want to take it with you, it is easy to do. As often happens a product will create the need for other products.

The solar tracking systems are a very good business. It is a tested engineered good product that we can sell with confidence. It did not just happen. First we designed the product and built a prototype. While enthused to begin selling it we realized that it was going to have some problems and we needed to find them and solve them prior to building them in quantity. We hired an engineer to review our product and give us specifications for foundations and the wind load calculations. For reasons of safety we wanted to use low voltage DC power for the required motors. During the first year we found out that our mechanical geometry moved the weight forward during the shortest days increasing the load on the motors, gears, chains. The cold weather made the grease in the gear box become thicker and increase loads. The movement by the controller required 30 seconds for each move. The very cold weather caused some controllers to fail. We realized that we needed to have the lubricant in the gearbox be of a lighter weight. We needed to change the geometry of the system to put it in balance so the load was always the same. We also realized the controller designed and built off shore did not use the quality components to work as well in all weather. We changed the gear ratios to move it in 1 minute and 20 seconds rather than 30 giving us 3 times the power. We had a reputable US manufacturer of electronics create a controller designed for all weather. Today we have a developed product that we are proud of. This does not happen without testing and real world experience. While the engineers are qualified and can do the math you must always be looking at ways to improve the product.

Because DH solar is a division of DH satellite we had the resources to build it and develop and improve it. The financial burden may have been too much for an undercapitalized startup company.

In the future, solar panels will be better and cheaper and the current electric cars with Lithium Ion batteries will make good batteries less expensive for home use. I forecast many residences will not need to be connected to the grid but rather make and store their own electricity. I also see the possibility that as the industry grows, some may choose to price the units too low and it could become a commodity product that is only profitable for the industry leaders with very large volume. I also see the possibility that solar panels will become so inexpensive the tracker is not worth its cost. Should others decide to sell at too low a price we are prepared to adapt or stop our interest in this product. I am sure that solar will be a big part of the future.

## Radio Stations

In the early years of our company I was always looking for opportunities. I was aware that there were few radio station frequencies available in the US. The government issued licenses for radio stations and spaced them so they did not interfere with each other. I also was aware that in Elkader in Clayton County, Iowa there was no radio station. It is the county seat. It was just across the Mississippi river from us so I thought I should try to start a station. It seems that people asked for those near larger cities and no one had ever applied for this radio station license.

I thought it might be a good business so I found the list of Radio station engineers and contacted one. I asked him to investigate to see if he could find a frequency that would work. He said yes and that the frequency would be 100.1 on the FM dial. Because of the spacing with others it would have to be 3000 Watts of power.

I authorized him to start the procedure to apply for this frequency; he made the application and we waited for the approval. By a coincidence at the same approximate time a young man who was a radio station engineer working in a station in Dubuque applied for it. This required us to compete for this frequency and it would take a while for the FCC to decide. The young many came to visit me and stated his life dream was to own his own station and that it was very important to him. I stated I wanted to do it because it would be fun and so I had made the application. Realizing how important it was to him I said I would withdraw but if he ever chose to sell it, to please contact me first. He was a fine young person and I wished him well.

To have a radio station you need to have an office for the program origination and a tower and transmitter. You have to choose the format you wish to broadcast and you need to have people to give the news and weather and program the music format.

A couple of years later he contacted me. He said he wanted to sell and quoted me a price. I agreed and we were in the radio business. He had applied for an AM license also so we had two radio stations with separate programming. It was a great fit. It worked well as we could advertise on our own station. We hired a manager and were pleased with the station.

As this was a rural area we chose country music as our format. We have a total of five full time employees and several part time employees. There is an office person, a news person, a backup news and commercial production person, and two sales people to sell ads. We found a very good, loyal audience, as the locals want to listen to the obituaries, the county board meeting information, the city council news, the local weather, and updates on severe weather. Local high school sports have a great audience and ads are an easy sell. We chose to purchase the music programming from a satellite source as they had the right mix of the latest music and some very professional announcers. They made a profit by having commercials run that they paid for. We had live programming from early in the morning with local news, weather and some national farm information such as crop and cattle pricing. Our AM station was playing the hits from the 50s and 60s eras and the commercial were placed into the computer controlled automation equipment. The program suppliers sent us many small audio clips with local mention and the audience thought the announcers were in the studio. We of course could interrupt at any time and be live. We have a van and an audio to studio link so we can do live broadcasts of special events, and when advertisers want to promote special events.

A few years passed and we became aware of a newer radio station in Iowa that was off the air. The people who started it had considerable debt and were unable to make the payments. It was available so we made an offer that was accepted; then we had three stations to run and sell ads. We had a manager that oversaw them and they did okay.

When we lost the manager, my son suggested that rather than hire a manager, why not have the stations run themselves. We could have a good set of books and pay the employees a percentage of the profits. His point was: if you were an owner operator you could run the stations well. Being the owner and not just the operator, if each person shared the income, they all would work hard to make it successful. If a sales person does not collect the receivables, an announcer will tell him to try harder. If I had it to do over, I would have purchased many rural radio stations and run them that way. I would not know how to run a big city station.

I worried that the satellite radio stations would take listeners away from us and the business may become a bad business. This is not the case. People want to know what happens in the community. They care about the city council meetings. They care about who died and about anything that is local news. They want concise local weather. It is a long term business.

New projects are fun. The most profitable thing is to do more of that which works, and that is OK but not as much fun.

## Honesty

Have you ever read about someone dishonest who goes to extremes to hide the dishonesty and puts so much effort into the con game project, that with the same effort he could have been successful?

I sold a truck load of scrap steel and not trusting the scrap buyer I double checked the weight slips and noticed that they paid me for the scrap and my truck. I called the junk dealer and said they made a mistake and he became angry. I then told him he paid me too much. He very quietly thanked me as I said I would send him the check.

I guess this is about our habits. In the big picture, dishonesty brings you little. Be honest.

I have a close friend that has said he has never told a lie; that his father and grandfather and he were in the military and they felt this honesty was important.

I have told many, many lies... and a few today. Nice car. Your hair looks good. What a nice looking motorcycle. While most of this was not an outright lie, it was a bit of an exaggeration and was done intentionally. While I might tell my wife her dress is nice but the other one is better. I really might think that it is awful, but I want to be nice. I have told an employee about all of their good traits, and then said they should probably work for a company that fits them better, and I was able to discharge them with fewer hard feelings.

In sales, what is really good and bad? Everything is a degree. Years ago I was very proud that we used three inches of wall insulation as my main competitor used only

1 ½ inches. I told how good that was. It was better but not good compared to today.

We buy rail cars of lumber. Most is SPF #2 and better. That allows a bit of "not-so-great." We pick the not-so-good out and use it for boxing antennas, and use the best for new homes. We say we have good lumber, and we do.

Do not cheat on your taxes. You are too young or too old to go to jail. Deduct it if it is business so you do not cheat yourself. If you push the limit, you may win the argument with the IRS, but do you want to be in a struggle fighting for something that fits the gray area. I have been audited, state and federal, for 40 years and find they are usually very good people. While an audit is not something you are pleased to hear about, when it is done you will have the comfort in knowing you do things pretty good, and while you many need to make an adjustment in depreciation or something, it is better to be careful than to worry that you are doing something totally wrong.

*No legacy is so rich as honesty.* Shakespeare 1619

## Businesses That Are Difficult

While many companies have been very successful selling a commodity, you probably will not. A commodity is best explained as a product on which you do not set the price. If you are selling lumber wholesale you can look up the current price and expect to be paid that. If you are manufacturing an item that is sold in very big quantity and many people have a similar product, you need to be competitive and cannot sell it at other than the standard price. Your markup is a major part of your success. As a bank director for many years I have, many times, seen a company fail with wonderful hard working and dedicated people that quote too low a price. Selling a commodity is great if you are the market leader, otherwise, not so good.

Big companies that sell a commodity will try to do "value added" to increase their margin of profit. When I began the company of spinning aluminum antennas I asked the two big manufacturers to sell me aluminum to spin on our machines into parabolic antennas. Both quoted me prices on circles they had created by rolling the coils to level, cutting a square, making a circle and selling it to me as a value added product. They charged a premium and kept the scrap. I could see in the Wall Street Journal the price of aluminum coil and I was paying a much higher price. I asked them both to sell me coil and they said at my large widths they could not do that. I took the ethical stand and lied to Alcoa; said I was buying coil stock from Reynolds; they told me to wait and then got back to me. They said I could buy coil. I then told Reynolds the same lie and I soon was buying a commodity at the lowest price. By cutting a circle from a coil I was able to have the 21% that was to be scrap and also buy at the lowest price. (an interesting side note: At the next IRS audit with sales of aluminum scrap at many hundreds of thousands of dollars they asked: "Where was the scrap income from the previous year?" I responded: "There was none.")

If you can weld and decide to go into a business you can decide "maybe I will buy steel, axles and hitches and make small trailers." There are many small companies that build trailers and they are efficient and buy in volume and sell in volume. Unless it is unique, it will be difficult to build, sell, and profit.

If instead you find you can manufacture a part that wears out on a *John Deere* Bulldozer and market it direct to the shop that fixes them, you will find that you can sell with a decent profit. *John Deere* will not have a low price and you may find a unique niche.

If you retail a product, manufacture a product, or import a product, find something you can do that makes you different. Then you can have "value added." It may be to avoid the normal marketing channels.

With our modular homes we sell direct to the consumer. The little dealer with a competitive product from a manufacturer has big overhead and usually pays interest on his investment. He is really not too efficient. He must have a higher price. We do things he cannot do. We can make changes. We use things that cost more money but give a consumer confidence. We use real 7-ply Douglas fir floor plywood rather than the normal OSB that is cheaper. Buying railroad car quantities saves money over truck loads. We put in more insulation and then make a deal to offer name brands. In our market, names like *Kohler, Lenox* and *Armstrong* are good names, we make them standard. By avoiding the dealers profit and inefficiency we can sell for a lower price but with a higher margin of profit. People like to buy direct and know they have better quality.

Sell something on the internet that has been sold in the past from a manufacturing company to a distributor who sold it to a dealer who retails it. You can have a great price and a great profit margin. For our satellite and solar division we purchased a 50 to 1 steel cased gear box with an input shaft and an output shaft. We thought it was made in Italy because it came from Italy. It had a machined part on it. We paid $380 for it and bought hundreds. While purchasing some items from China I came upon an identical gear box; I assumed it was going to Italy and then to the US where a jobber added the part and sold it to our supplier. I started buying it in China; it is identical and we have used many hundreds. They made the adapter and the cost is $44 plus $8 for the adapter.

I wanted a message sign out in front of our retail store and checked with China and got a quote. I had a US quote for the sign, not installed, for $9000. The quote from China was $800. I quickly ordered two to be air freighted. My employees said "you are taking a chance as it may be no good." We plugged it in and it worked with our company logo, time and temperature. I asked our experienced computer guy to put a message on it and the software was in Chinese. No one within 100 miles could understand it but we followed up with China; they forwarded the English software. A young person with a little cash could buy a half container of them, put a trailer behind his car and go down the road selling those signs for $2500, and he could continue until *Sam's Club* stared selling them for $1200.

What does it take in the simplest terms? Maybe first, self-confidence. Create goals and plans to achieve them and know you can do it. A desire, hard work—but not extreme—be thinking all the time, be looking at things and how they are made. Be looking for the newest and better way. The internet is today full of growth and new ways to market. Be on the lookout for the opportunities and make your move. I have never failed to pay a legitimate bill. I have never stolen anything. Have I guessed wrong and lost money? Of course. You create a better life going slow and steady, build net worth, and build on it. Buying your first new car on credit can cause you to never make it big. Wait for the net worth and then buy a Mercedes and enjoy it.

Most small business that you can purchase or start are not going to be better than a job. You need a unique business to have the success you want. You can start a small shoe store but maybe you are just creating a bad job. Buying container loads of hammers in China and selling them to hardware stores may be a wonderful job.

Often people will lose their job and decide it is time to go into business for themselves. They enjoy a beer or three and maybe they should buy a tavern. It might be fun for a while and can be successful, but there is a big strain on the marriage. Often the exposure to the drinking can cause the owner to drink too much. It is hard to keep control and usually, unless it is a unique business in a unique location, maybe it is just buying a bad job.

The failure rate on restaurants is terribly high. Banks are very concerned as the percentage of new mom and pop restaurants that fail in the first few years is considerable.

*Failure is contagious.* Don Tweedy 2012

## Work Habits

We all are the result of our habits. Why do you put the same shoe on first each day? Because it is your habit. If you have a habit of stealing and you see an opportunity and do not take it, you probably would feel guilty. If you develop the habit of accomplishing something every day and a day goes by without an accomplishment, you will feel guilty.

If I see something new, I need to see if it is cast, forged, machined, molded, cut from a computer controlled plasma torch, or laser cut and then shaped. Could it be better? Could I make it at a profit? Then, if I could, do I want to?

We build our habits. If you exercise every day, and then miss a day, you will feel guilty. If you drink 9 beers every night, you will want the same tomorrow night. If you kiss your wife and tell her you love her every day, it will be difficult to go to bed without making the call.

There are good habits and bad habits. Recognize this and try to develop the good ones.

I feel guilty if I miss the evening news, as it is my habit to watch it. I feel guilty if I do not accomplish something every day.

Lists are important. I have pads with lists. I also had pads with lists when I was 40 years younger. The lists are: (1) long term accomplishments; (2) short term accomplishments; (3) today's list.

I carry a note pad, and I did when I was younger with a better memory. This is so I can make a note of what I want to do and what to add to my lists.

When I air travel commercially and have time, I have a pad and paper and write down:

Each division
House building
Radio station marketing and production
Rental units
Retailing
Rental apartments
Mortgage Company

Then I start to make myself notes of what I can do to improve them. How should we change things? How should we market? Direct mail? Email? Phone calls? Newspaper ads? TV? Billboards?

What kind of promotion can we make to generate more business?

I enjoy commercials to see if I can learn something we can do. I like to look at retail business's ads to see what we can learn.

**Self-confidence:** You have to convince yourself you can achieve anything you want, if you do not believe you will fail. If you really wanted to, you could learn to play the piano excellently. You could be a great athlete if you worked at it.

**Practice:** You will not be the fun person who can play the piano unless you make the effort and stick to it. There are no natural musicians; they all need a real interest and practice. Tiger practiced at golf a lot.

*I do not know the secret to success but the secret to failure is trying to please everyone.* Bill Cosby 1980

## What if you do not like your job?

I used to watch the clock and I wanted it to hurry during school. At work I often discover it was time to go home an hour ago. Work should and can be great, satisfying fun.

Now maybe your job it is not great and less then you expect. Try to change it for the better. Ask for some way to make it enjoyable and *you and your employer* will win.

If you cannot quit because you need the income, continue and start a part time project that can grow to be your own employment. You can work 20 hours a week in your spare time if it can mean great success in the future. (Also the work habit might make you more successful in the future.)

If you apply for a job, do some planning. Go well dressed and be upbeat and positive. Do not hesitate to promise "I will be dependable and not be late to work; I am honest and will work hard to make your business a success."

I am amazed that people will apply for a job with their tattoos exposed and wearing dirty clothes. You may not be eloquent in your speaking, so practice your job application.

Why do you feel you do not like your job? Can the job be changed? Some people really do not fit certain jobs. I had a farmer working in our company as a supervisor and he was a great worker and a great supervisor. He owned a dairy farm and told me several times "I love to milk the cows at night. I look forward to it and it is a peaceful time for me." As a child we had cows and no electricity so we had to milk them by hand. I hated it and looked forward to the time I could leave the cows. When you build a wall you can stand it up and look at it. When you milk a cow you have to do it again in the morning. I said that if given a choice between milking cows for life or going to jail for a few years I would take the jail and enjoy the rest of life. If you cannot adapt, I guess you need to make plans to quit and find something you love.

*If you love what you do, you never have to go to work. Real success is finding your life work in something you love.* McCullough

## How Much to Mark Up a Product

I have told young business people this story many times, and now, sometimes, I believe it is true. It is not true but it is interesting: My Norwegian grandfather talked about profit and margins to me and said Grandson, "you do not need a big profit to be successful, and One percent is enough if you do volume. If it cost you a dollar and you sell it for two dollars, be satisfied with one percent markup". Of course this is 100 percent but a pretty good way to mark it up. As I hope you know, if you markup Grandfathers 1 percent (100 percent) your percentage is 50% gross markup on sales. Not hard to have a good ending net, but very hard to sell at this kind of markup.

When I started my company *Design Homes* I knew what I was going to build and I knew what the materials would cost. I had a good estimate of what the labor would be and I knew there would be items called overhead that would be added. I wanted to make a net profit of 10% on gross sales and I wanted to print a price list of the three plans I wanted to market. I had built the model and knew the costs. I figured the numbers many times and then added 10% as my hoped-for margin of profit. I took the numbers to the printer, because there were no copy machines in 1966, and at the last minute changed the markup to 20 percent. At the end of each month I prepared a balance sheet and at the end of the year I put together the numbers. Depreciation was something that you can actually write off quicker than the things go down in value, so I made the balance sheet for me and my bank's information using real value, and when I was done, I made 10% on sales. I reviewed the costs of electricity and all those variables and the end number was still 10 percent. As I tell young business people when I checked to see where the other 10 percent went, I was unable to find it. It was just gone. The lesson from this, had I marked it up 10 percent and showed the bank that I lost money on paper, figuring depreciation, but also, that I really lost money, and that I did not create positive cash flow. They would have politely said they were not going to extend my loan. There are unknowns and my recommendation is to keep an adequate profit margin, or if that is not possible, get out of the business.

Many businesses by their nature do not have a good markup but can be profitable if the volume is great.

When the company was doing many small installations of satellite systems, we would purchase the small F connecter used in coax cable. We paid 9.5 cents apiece. I recently went to a radio shack store and purchased two (you cannot buy one) and it was $2. I thought "Wow! They buy right and that is a really big markup." Thinking it over, they had clerks ring it up and do paper work, so my ideas that most things should have a reasonable markup may be correct after you take in selling costs. Maybe my percentage thinking is wrong for some products.

As a bank director I have seen many good people go into a business and work hard and think hard work is the key to success. It sure helps and it is difficult to be successful without hard work, but it is less important than pricing the product right. It is truly sad to see the failure because they did not take an adequate markup and worked very hard— all for nothing.

When building my first home I needed a water heater. I stopped at a plumbing shop and talked to the owner who became a great friend. He showed me a water heater and quoted me his price. He stated, "This is my cost". I said "Seymour, how can you sell me a water heater at your cost?" He said, "I buy at less than cost."

## Understanding a Balance Sheet

At school you were exposed accounting and to a balance sheet and a statement of earnings. You were day dreaming probably about cars or boys or something and did not pay much attention. A balance sheet is something we should all do until our assets are so large and so many it is too much work and you can hire others to do it.

Even if you do not have a business you should create a balance sheet and compare it with last year.

In its simplest terms a balance sheet shows your assets and liabilities. The difference is your net worth or lack of same. Say you sold popcorn at a stand and each month created a balance sheet it might say:

March 1, Alice's popcorn stand:

| Assets | | Liabilities | |
|---|---|---|---|
| popcorn | $150 | wholesaler bill due | $200 |
| | | | |
| bags | $8 | | |
| salt | $3 | | |
| oil | $140 | oil bill due | $22 |
| popcorn stand | $1,200 | Grandpa for stand | $800 |
| prepaid insurance | $200 | wages due | $44 |
| | | net worth | $635 |
| total | $1,701 | total | $1,701 |

It balances. If you do this every month you will see the growth of net worth or the loss you have created. I kept a monthly balance sheet for the first several years. While I could properly write off some things faster than the value declined, I showed real value as it was only for me and my banker to see.

The growth of the net worth is the profit you made and it is good to know what is happening. The statement of earnings is only showing how you got there. I sold $?? and I spent $?? and the ending statement was my balance sheet.

As a bank director I have been reviewing large loan applications as part of the loan committee. When you prepare your bank statement with a balance sheet, do not try to fool yourself or your banker. If you have an 8 year old Ford pickup you use in your business and a new one sells for $25,000, and you list your truck as worth $20,000, they will suspect the value of everything you listed as wrong. Try to list everything reasonably. Otherwise, they may decide they do not want to do business with you.

Another thing to remember is that your interest rate on a loan and your ability to get a loan is by your credit score. The credit score is real and looked at often in financial circles. I made $20 on a bet once when the bank I work for discussed credit scores; I said, "I bet my score is less than a friend with a good net worth, but much less than mine." Credit scores do not reflect your net worth. (I think they should) They reflect your credit history. Usually a high credit score means the person pays all bills promptly and is a good credit risk. A credit score over 800 is very good and the lowest I have seen is 350. If you are above 700 you are looking pretty good. The national average is 710. My score was less than the guy that used a credit card a lot more. My wife has a higher credit score then mine.

This book wanders a lot as you may have noticed. As I

talk of credit scores I want to also talk about borrowing. Avoid it as much as you can. Amortize it as short as you can and argue for a lower rate whatever it is. Real strength is to be debt free and have a cushion of cash. You will be able to live through the rough times when others fail.

## Financial

Anticipate inflation. My plan of long term and getting wealthy slowly means you will see periods of little inflation and big inflation. I built 85 rental units early in my career. I thought that this was financial strength as they could be rented. If there was inflation they would grow in value with inflation. They were built when a new Chevy sedan was $3000 and today the equivalent car would be $22,000. Inflation means your inventory is going up in value. It also means if you sell something in March and deliver it in November you might lose money. It is real; anticipate it.

Warren Buffet says cash is a poor investment, as its value goes down because of inflation. He also said "I keep enough cash to sleep well."

History shows my net worth would have been greater had I kept less cash and more growth investments. I do not care, as I have slept well.

If you have the interest and time and are very thorough, you can review all common stocks and come up with some bargains that are underpriced and high quality. You can purchase and hold these and see them grow to become very valuable. You do not pay taxes until you sell so you can see your net worth grow with tax paid only on the sale.

Warren Buffet has said buy quality and hold. Do not speculate. Do not buy and sell and try to be a day trader as you will create a taxable event each time you sell for a profit; tax payments leave you less to invest.

Do not try to be a day trader as *almost no one* has

made money that way. Every time you take a profit you create a taxable event. The person who bought what you sold is probably smarter then you are. There are many very smart people in the market. If you do not have the time or interest in picking your own stocks, find an index fund and invest. Historically the market has grown and will continue. With pending inflation it will go up faster sometime in our near term future, and extra cash is best left in an index fund.

I have a friend who uses a brokerage firm that is big and expensive. He loves them as they make a profit for him. He said they have purchased ATT seven times and always made a profit for him. That is a true statement and that is a great company. My unspoken thought was you would have been much better off using a discount broker, buying it once and holding it. Each sale costs a commission and each sale was profitable, so it created a taxable event.

## Perceived value

Is price important? Of course it is and that is proven by the fact that *Walmart* is the largest marketer in the world and does the most business in dollars and has so many employees. They promote the low prices.

I guess my next question should be, "Is low price always the most important factor to a purchaser?" Not always, and if you can take advantage of this, you can be more profitable in whatever business you choose.

An example is the *Gibralter* satellite commercial antenna story:

We started to lose market share on antennas in the mid 1980s. We chose to go to the worldwide markets that were a higher frequency and needed more accurate antennas. As this market grew I became aware of the commercial market that was large antennas that were mostly fiberglass, heavy and not so good. I decided to make antennas for the commercial market. I made the world's biggest spinning machine and made a 5 meter antenna, 16' 4". It worked great and I planned to be successful in this market.

I made a polar tracking mount and hauled my first product to Las Vegas to the broadcast convention. I set it up in the parking lot and it received a lot of attention. Every one visited and took a brochure; I was enthused until the show was over and I had no orders.

My aluminum antennas and mount cost us about $1200 at that time and so I priced it at $3,000. The competitors had 5 meter fiberglass that were not as good and they were offered at $5,995.00. I wondered why my antennas did not sell! The TV stations engineers were employees of big corporations with executives that wanted perfection and the engineers did not want to buy the cheap one and maybe have problems and be in trouble. They wanted quality and they equated that with price.

A year later I came to the show with my *"Gibralter"* It was so over built I was almost embarrassed. It was priced at $9,995.00. It tracked the azimuth and the elevation, each separately. It cost more but the engineer knew it would not move in the wind. It was possible for him to motor it onto a satellite, go back and forth, then up and down and be exactly in the center of the satellite signal both ways. It was expensive but it was solid.

Today over 30 years later DH satellite (dhsatellite.com) is a primary supplier to cable companies, Nexrad radar sites, ship board satellite reception, universities, military and many other uses of parabolic antennas.

In creating this perceived value it is important to use name brands. Is the *Kohler* toilet really better than a much cheaper one? I am not sure, but I will pay the extra to have the *Kohler* name. Usually our company can commit to a minimum of 600 toilets and in negotiations with *Kohler*, we do get a great price and it is probably about the same as our competitors that always use the lowest price stuff.

Is more insulation better? Yes. How much should you use, then? There is a diminishing return, as if you had no insulation and put in 2 inches it would be much better. If you changed that to 4 inches it would be a lot better, but not twice as good. We have 14 inches in our ceilings with an R value of 50; our competitors chose to use the code minimum of R 38. It all helps our image and helps us sell more homes.

Sometimes we find new products are less expensive and better, as well. For years we promoted copper water lines. They cost more than plastic but everyone knows it is better. Well, copper is not perfect, either, and the newest piping of plastic is really better. That's where the sales person comes to explain to the customers.

It is a high margin business and the antennas sell well for the same reason my wife will not buy me a shirt at *Walmart.* It is perceived value.

## Charity

We give a substantial amount to charities each year and we also have a will for major contributions when we die.

The "meals on wheels" program is great, furnishing meals to elderly at a moderate cost. If you know of people who are in need, just contact the supplier and agree to pay for them. It is a modest amount and it creates a good feeling helping the needy.

I have a friend who contacted a grade school and asked the principal if any kids needed winter jackets. They said yes and gave a list of sizes needed. He bought them and told me about it. The principal mentioned a young boy who was so happy that it was his, and that he could take it home; he began to cry.

We then started contacting schools and asking the same questions. In one school, the teacher said all the kids should get one, as most are in need, but she did not want to embarrass them. We did. The person giving the gift is rewarded by the good feeling.

When I see a billboard promoting a charity, I feel that I do not want to give to them and pay for more bill boards. I want to pay to accomplish the charities goals.

Some charities spend most of the money paying professionals to try to collect more money. There have been executives staying in Five Star hotels, using limos and being paid high salaries. I do not want to give to them.

Because of a personal loss we have been making big contributions to a church account that gives money to people attending school beyond high school. There are no operating costs and the account pays out all the interest and a small amount of principal each year. This has been going on for 35 years, and now it has a very big balance. This can continue long after we are gone.

## The Most Fun Project of My Life

About 15 years ago at a Thanksgiving dinner in a discussion of fun things to do, someone in the family said it would be fun to buy a farm and build a golf course. Someone else said that when it was done it would be fun to own, and if we sold lots off the golf course, we would maybe have a free golf course. The discussion continued and soon the idea developed into a plan. The question was "where to build it?" We knew our local town had a nice golf course, and being a small town with two golf courses, neither would do well. We needed population.

We all agreed we would look for a farm that would make a good golf course, buy the farm, do the needed zoning, buy the equipment and build it ourselves. We looked and looked and looked and felt that maybe La Crosse or Dubuque would be the place, but both had developments in the works. The biggest market was the state capital, Madison.

Madison is the location of the University of Wisconsin. The county has a population of over 500,000 people and is growing. We felt it always could use another golf course. It is in Dane county which has a reputation for being extremely liberal. Our past efforts to purchase land and build a home display had been stopped by the zoning and bureaucrats. Iowa County joined Dane county and was rural and seemed like the place to build. It was only a half hour drive from Madison.

I asked my friend who ran our bank about a farm and he said, pick one out and I will foreclose! (A bit of banker's humor). He called a banker in the area and the banker mentioned a 400 acre dairy farm that was for sale. It was ideal as it had a mile of 4 lane highway exposure. It was at the edge of Barneveld, Wisconsin.

We looked, we loved it, and we bought it. It is almost 400 acres. We asked for zoning changes and it was quickly approved. It is a rocky farm and some areas could not be plowed so those areas were left as pasture. Being a larger ratio of pasture, the farm had areas of violet plants.

The Regal Fritillary butterfly is endangered and likes violets. We were told by the state DNR butterfly lady we could not build a golf course. We made a deal, we would make efforts to not disturb the butterfly and would try to keep its habitat as it was. We agreed we would not plant leafy trees in its area and we would do burning as the DNR asked. We also agreed for ten years we would let them keep track of the butterflies. We kept our word and many people come just to see the butterflies.

There are many deer, so our family named it *Deer Valley Golf Course*. The course has a valley in its center and with the elevation changes is very beautiful.

We walked it and hit golf balls and thought about the many ways to lay out a golf course. We bought a used dump truck; we bought a *John Deere* crawler dozer with a six way blade. We bought a *Cat* dozer D6 (more fun than any airplane). We bought some tractors and other equipment and applied for the erosion control permit from the state. We removed fences and started to stake a layout. The plan has the clubhouse very visible in the center.

We mowed a 2000 foot area to land the Piper Seneca twin engine airplane and started to fly to the site. It would take 20 minutes with the Seneca, and an hour and 20 minutes with a pickup truck, so flying saved about two hours a day. Besides... its fun.

We began laying out the first nine holes going up a hill with a long par five that was very visible from the highway. Three par four holes going along the ridge and then the signature hole—a par three that is about 90 feet higher than the green. The shot is only about 100 yards over water and most people hit too much club the first time. Then a winding road down to the green (few people walk it) then a par four back up the hill, a par three, a long par five, and then from the ridge a beautiful hole to finish the nine back to the clubhouse. The back nine is similar coming back to the club house on a second ridge with a big valley in the center.

Between me and my son, we agreed on the layout and began shaping dirt. We did it all except contracting for the irrigation. We read all the books on golf course building and design and tried to take the advice to make it appear difficult but to play a bit easier.

Did we make mistakes? Yes, as expected. We did not compact the tees enough or make them large enough. Later when they settled we had to redo them to be larger and level.

My wife was concerned about the beauty of it and wanted decorative rocks placed with flower beds. For the first few years she would plant the flowers. I would work on it every Tuesday and every Friday and often Saturday and Sunday. My son would put in a day or two each week running heavy equipment. My Grandson was there helping every chance he could.

My Granddaughter, Amber, would always try to spend at least one day a week with Grandpa helping on the course. She was in high school and would arrive at my office at 8 AM; we would go to the airport. She would help push the Seneca out and check the airplane. Then we would get in and she would start the engines, taxi it to the end of the runway, and then take off and fly us to the golf course. At our short grass strip, I would land the plane, and then we would work on a fun project. If we were building a mound, I would run a loader and she would drive the dump truck. Before we would leave we would play nine holes. We would talk about politics, business, boys and life, and then I would start the Seneca and take off. She would fly home and land.

She became captain of the golf team in high school. She continued helping me though college and by the time she graduated, we had built a hotel and banquet facility; she took charge of the hotel and banquet operation. She is now married and with her husband, is still running the hotel and banquet operation.

Our first 18 holes are par 36 for each nine holes, for a par 72 course. A large, wild valley separated the two nine holes. We had a very difficult course to play. Scratch golfers love long difficult holes, but they are not the majority. After a few years while working on a project, I talked to an older gentleman who told me he really loved the course because of the scenery, but because it was so difficult, he only played once a year.

I discussed this with the golf professional who is the general manager and he said he would talk to some of the regular golfers and see if it should be any easier. They all said "leave it alone... we love it." My experience was that I lost a lot of golf balls and really thought it was a difficult course. My next project was to mow much wider as many golfers slice, and this deep rough area mowed allowed them to find the ball and hit again. Next, knowing most golfers are right handed and slice, we built some mounds on the right side that will often deflect a ball back into the fairway. The course became a bit easier and the sale of new golf balls went down. Golfers like a good score. They really like it better.

The golf course is a financial success mostly because the management takes great care of the events and promotes golf events for corporations. This meant that some of the good regular golfers could not play when there was an event. We talked about building a third nine holes. Knowing the population is becoming older we all decided to make this a par 35 nine holes. We went for larger greens, and using the land in the valley and the sides of the hills, we designed a course that has six of the nine holes much elevated from the fairways and greens. This makes an average golfer hit further. We left rough areas between the tees and the fairways that were easy to hit over because the tees were elevated. We made the greens larger and easier to hit. Often there is a long cart path between the green and the next hole, so we encourage using a golf cart.

Today the third nine has its own following. Many people request it. I have never played it without losing a golf ball, and I know it's because I swing too hard. I love the entire course, but I prefer the front nine and the center nine. Someday I will leave my driver at home and hope to play it without losing a ball.

The finish hole of the third nine is over 300 yards but sloping down some. It has a tree about one hundred yards in front of the green and a sand trap in front. It is aligned with the prevailing winds and as it slopes a bit, it is tempting for good golfers to try to drive the green. I left a $100 bill with the golf pro and said the first league player to drive the green gets this. It lasted one day. A golfer drove the green.

Family is what made this "the funnest thing in my life."

The return on investment is not great. I do not really care.

We did NOT sell the lots to make the course no cost to us. Someone may, someday when I am gone, but I really do not want houses on our golf course.

My instructions for when I die are: "Please scatter my ashes on the golf course, except hole number 12." I cannot par 12 and I do not like it.

What also has been great about *Deer Valley Golf* is that it is never done. You can always do something else to make it prettier or better. While the golf course is now 13 years old, I have been doing new projects every year.

The golf industry is not doing wonderful. In the North Country you have a short season and people will not play golf when:

When it is cold

When it is raining

When it is hot

When it is windy

When it is forecast to be bad

Land is expensive and it is expensive to build a course.

It is expensive to maintain them in excellent condition.

The conclusion is: perhaps it is not smart to build a golf course only as an investment. Our golf course is paid for and profitable, but more than that, it was fun to build and is fun to improve and fun to own. I have golf events with friends every year and love to be there.

As a bank director I am often looking at business plans. To build a hotel on a golf course without a city does not make much sense. But if you want to do it, and you can afford to do it, and are willing to work hard, you can make it a success. We decided to build a 62 room hotel with a water park and a very large area of meeting rooms and a banquet room.

Deer Valley Lodge on the 400 acre Deer Valley Golf Course
12,000 sq ft water park, 62 room hotel and banquet room

Deer Valley Golf pro shop

View of the rolling hills of the beautiful 27 hole Golf course

*Isaac Newton would have difficulty explaining why a golf ball hit easily goes farther than one hit hard.*
Frank Weeks

## Advertising

Ya gotta.
Can you directly measure its effectiveness? No.
What are the kinds of advertising?

Personal contact, stop and see the prospects.
TV
Radio
Newspaper
Shoppers
Billboards
Signs
Hand out sheets
Exotic blimps, sky writing, etc.

I always admired the Volkswagen ads of years ago. So funny you would laugh out loud. How does the snow plow driver get to the snow plow?

Wendy's! Where is the beef?

When you have a short time to tell a long story and are not well known your best ad is to promote your features. If you have none, you should not be in the business.

At our radio stations there has been a car dealer that would put on eight ads a day for four days and then be off for two weeks. People would comment that he was on all the time. Interesting.

In our very early days of *Design Homes* I purchased a small series of ads on Rochester, Minnesota TV. Within two weeks we had two new sales in Rochester; I was ecstatic. I felt I knew how to sell as many homes as I wanted. Pick a new or old location and run some TV ads. A month later I again ran a bigger run of spots in Rochester and sold nothing. Then 6 months later some people who had seen the ad and planned a new home on retirement came in and bought a home.

Advertising is hard to measure—but necessary.

Another source of advertising is to keep your customers happy. We have a local family with five children and we have sold them five new homes.

We had a person in our town that ran a small business and bought an early home from us that was three bedroom, one bath, very modest 1000 sq. ft. home. Soon he realized he could afford a bigger home for his growing family and ordered a larger home with bigger rooms, two baths and a larger garage. When his family grew he had us build a three bedroom with a den, split foyer home with a large lower level recreation room. As the family left home they decided to build a log loft home with a view on a hillside. Later they sold that and retired in the south and could tell people that every home they purchased was sold for a profit. Had we not done a good job on the first home, we would have lost several sales. That, too, is advertising.

Word of mouth is always good advertising.

We started business in 1966 and as we grew in size we were contacted by the Internal Revenue Service that we would be audited. The first audit is stressful and you are not sure you really are doing everything right. The auditor found some errors that were corrected, and the end of the audit was pleasant. The auditor left the IRS a few years later, joined an accounting firm in the North part of the state and returned to order a new home. The exposure to our operation resulted in a sale.

We have used billboards and we felt they were successful. We have used newspapers and we felt they were very good. We use an informational ad that we put on the internet and TV and that is excellent. We always use radio and know that works.

Effectiveness of advertising is hard to measure, but it is certainly necessary.

## Success

What is success and how do we achieve it? Financial freedom is really being able to truly live a successful life. Good health which we have some control over; enjoying your work, enjoying your free time; building a loving family that you are proud of and enjoy; having good friends and fun hobbies—this is success.

(At my age I feel I'm like my grandfather so I repeat myself often.) Develop good habits. Feel guilty if you are not productive. Be thinking all the time and looking for opportunities. Put in efforts to avoid problems. Avoiding problems is more important than maximum profits. Be proud that you are honest. Be loving and caring and you will be treated the same way. Be considerate of infirm and unfortunate. Gain the great good feeling of giving to efficient charity.

Today I have family that runs day to day business operations. Someday I will be gone and so by spending time away I feel I am enjoying my hobbies, and at the same time preparing them for business without me.

Part of success has been to accumulate net worth to give me peace of mind. If you have paid for apartments that generate rent income without debt, that will give you peace of mind. Land that is rented for a good return will give you peace of mind. Business ventures that cash flow and generate income will give you peace of mind. Cash in the bank in CDs and money market instruments will give you peace of mind.

Also important are your hobbies. I love golf, but I become less proficient each year. I expect to continue playing and trying to be better, even though I expect I will not become better. It will be a sad day when I cannot play any longer. I have always loved and collected cars and I will continue. I enjoy restoring them and making an old car better. They increase in value but that is not the motive. I will never sell them. I enjoy flying. The speed to get someplace and then back is important, but there is more to it than that. It is a thrill. To take a world war two veteran for a scenic ride in my old army airplane is great. To fly the jet as it accelerates on takeoff is a thrill.

## My product failure - The hot glue machine

In about 1970 we had a busy and great year building modular homes. We had an order back log and were working at capacity. I had a partial night shift operating and was looking for any method we could find to become more efficient.

I was buying better equipment such as saws and air operated nailing equipment, and anything that would speed up production. We installed I beams in the ceiling of the factory with electric hoists that could pick up large and heavy loads and move them around.

Our home building system worked because of the extra strength in the walls we could achieve by gluing everything we nailed. By gluing the side wall sheathing we had much greater strength than just nailing. The nailing would make it strong but there was a bit of give when stress was on the walls. As we bought glue in 55 gallon drums we found that gluing the floor plywood down even increased the strength of the home.

One day a supplier mentioned to me that the way we glued things looked pretty primitive to him. We had employees take a pail of glue and a brush and put the glue on the wall studs and the floor joists. He said that some people had a pump to install the glue where needed.

I was aware of a company that had also placed a small steel wire along the top of the floor joists and when they applied the glue they connected the wires to electricity to make them hot as I understand hot glue is better than just glue.

At that time I wrongly thought I was a real smart person and that I should invent a way to apply glue that was less labor intensive than using a pail and a brush. I had recently had a 55 gallon water heater that had a dent in it so we could not include it with a new home.

I had the "eureka moment"—why not fill the tank with glue, put a hose with a nozzle on it, and put air pressure to the tank. I filled it with glue and put on air pressure and out of the nozzle came glue that I could then just apply as needed. I was sure I was the smartest person in town. I personally applied the glue to a floor system and was very pleased.

As I thought about it some more I realized that the water heater tank had heating elements in it. I could plug in the electricity and I would have a "hot glue machine."

I asked the guys to connect power and they did. It was lunch time and so I stayed and talked to the workers while the hot glue machine was warming up.

When it exploded the noise was deafening. The bottom of the tank was still on the floor, but the water heater became a rocket. It went straight up and struck a steel ceiling I-beam that was used to pick up walls and floors with an electric hoist. Much of the water heater was fastened to the beam which was destroyed. The roof truss was destroyed and needed to be replaced. Parts of it went through the roof and were never found. 52 gallons of glue was spread all over the factory. The factory had four furnaces that had pilot lights that were blown out.

Thankfully, no one was hurt. While this happened 40 years ago, I still get guys laughing and commenting about my "hot glue machine."

What happened was the glue was not like water to circulate but rather the area close to the heating element turned to steam and of course I did not have a pressure relief valve installed.

It was a big joke to so many people but the good news is no one was hurt. People could have been injured or killed. I was careless and stupid.

As a young company we had a wonderful gentleman named Leo who came out of retirement to help me. He had business experience and he was doing all the materials purchasing and many other duties. A stray dog had stopped to visit us at the plant and the guys would feed him at lunch time and so Leo kind of adopted the dog. As Leo did the purchasing often something would not be available and Leo would explain that the item was "back ordered." Soon Leo's dog was named Backorder. Backorder was everyone's friend in the plant.

When the hot glue machine blew up, Backorder ran away and did not come back for several days. He must have thought we had a dangerous place.

What is the lesson? The lesson is look for possibly dangerous situations and be careful. It would be easy to leave the cover off an electrical panel and have someone become electrocuted. It would be possible to have a truck with bad brakes cause an accident. I have found workers using a forklift truck that had brake failures. The lesson is being careful and still too many things can happen.

How do we apply glue today 40 years later? With a pail and a brush.

## Salesmanship

We think of a sales person as the one at the car dealership trying to sell you something you do not want, or the guy knocking on the door with a vacuum cleaner in his hand. Salesmanship is a very important thing in your life and you should work to develop it.

You may not think of it that way but successful people in all walks of life are the best salespersons. You sell yourself to your spouse to make you both happy. You sell yourself to your boss and your friends. You convince your friend to go with you to the football game and that is selling. If you sell yourself to the kids they like you and will not want to disappoint you. Their behavior will be better. We all sell all the time. It makes living better.

I do not mean we all are marketing a product and trying to sell it. If you are a doctor you sell your patient on following your instructions so they get better. If you are a coach you sell the team on working hard and practicing. If you are a preacher you sell your faith to the congregation. If you are a politician you try to sell yourself to the people so they vote for you.

Communications is part of salesmanship. To be successful you need to be a good communicator. I find that emails are so much better than phone calls. For one thing they result in things in writing so there is no excuse that I did not understand. The phone call often starts with a discussion of the Green Bay Packers and the weather. A phone call often finds the other person gone, a message left, and you're busy or away when the call is returned. I often have made a tour of the facilities to visit with people and follow up with my requests in writing.

You all have made many purchases in your life. You like to make a big purchase from someone you like.

Some selling hints:

Make the customer like you

Have product knowledge

Tell your features

Repeat your features again (they may not have been listening)

Explain your advantages

Never bring up the competition (When competition is brought up, show you have product knowledge. In response I might say: "They are good people who build a good product but we..."

Then shut up and listen to the customer!!!!

Ask some questions and listen to the answers

Learn what is important to the customer

Ask for the order or what you want

Try to do the person you are selling to a favor. Offer to check something out for them. Draw them a sketch and mail it.

In selling a home, start and finish every visit with your features. We sell direct; we use more insulation; we include more.

When people come in to our sales location and start looking at homes and you approach them and say "can I help you," 90% will say, "No, just looking."

If I say "We sell our homes factory direct and custom

build to order. We can save you money selling direct as we deliver and complete it including everything except the land, basement and utility connections. We include the furnace installed and pay the state's tax on the home."

By then you need to take a breath and they always ask a question. You have a dialogue going.

Keep a record and follow up: A letter, a phone call, an email.

Stop and see the customer in person and ask if there is anything you can do to help.

## Accumulate Wealth with Minimum Taxes

Buy quality growth stocks and hold them until you die and you created net worth (the growth in value). You pay no taxes until or when you sell it and then at a lower capital gains rate. Public companies often pay dividends and that is taxable income.

Depreciation is real. If you buy something for business you can depreciate it for its life. I bought a new airplane that I could properly depreciate in 5 years. It was expensive and its value on the books was fully depreciated to no value in a short time. It is and was a great airplane and the new ones went up in price. I had created a great net worth without yet paying taxes on it and when sold, it would be at the lower capital gains rate. The government wants businesses to buy new things to create employment. There is no loser.

**The 1031 exchange:** It is possible to delay taxes by selling a thing, a rental unit, an airplane, whatever, and applying the gain towards the new one. I had a Beech King Air airplane that was very valuable but had no value on the books. I sold it and the funds were held in a special 1031 account and then applied to a new aircraft. I did not have to recapture the gain. This is reasonable for the government to allow as it creates more sales. It is something to take advantage of. You could build a duplex for $100,000 and when it is valued at $200,000 sell it, and if you put the funds into the 1031 exchange program, you delay paying the tax on the gain. If you find another apartment you want, you can use the funds to pay on it and delay any income tax until you dispose of that property. It then changes the basic cost of the new one.

**Capital gains taxes:** Buy an investment property and hold it the proper time and you are taxed on it at capital gain rate. Today that is 15% and a lot better than the normal rate. If you choose to purchase an apartment and later in life choose to sell it, any gain over your costs (purchase price less depreciation) is taxed at that rate. While people will argue that income earned by investments should not pay less taxes than income earned by working there is a reason for it. When the tax rate on capital gains went down I made many property sales and paid taxes. I would not have made the sale if it had been the higher rate.

If you built rental houses that cost $100,000 each, did all the work yourself, and the materials and land cost you $40,000, you have created a net worth gain of $60,000 without taxes at that time, but rather when you sell. You could take the materials (not the land) and begin depreciating it. Build ten of them and keep them rented until you are old and then sell them and pay a capital gain tax. You are a millionaire, and if you die owning them you never paid tax on that part. You did on the rent. (I hope)

Why do so many people move to Texas or Nevada when they get old and wealthy? They properly do not have to pay state taxes on unearned income. They move in droves from New York and New Jersey to states like Nevada and Florida and others without state income taxes.

Create a revocable trust. There is no tax advantage but you function as an individual but have the trust with you as the trustee. When you die a new trustee takes over and there is no probate. Simple and easy to do and avoids a lot of costs and time for your family. If you're net worth becomes considerable, talk to professionals about nonrevocable trusts, as they may help your estate planning.

The lawyer I worked with on estate planning told me about an interesting situation. A 94 year old lady was the matriarch of a large family that had older children running five corporations. She had done no estate planning and this was a time of $1,000,000 personal exemption and 55% tax. The family had to sell assets of four of the corporation to allow one to survive. Had she made plans 30 years prior she could have done annual gifting and let corporation ownership be shared and it would have reduced this tax burden. The unfairness is because those very wealthy with the top law firms are able to reduce or eliminate the taxes on billionaires. The hard working farmer that did not do estate planning can have the farm sold to pay these taxes rather than let the children own and run it.

I am aware of many successful businesses that continue to operate as "C" corporations with double taxation rather than making the change to "Sub S" or "LLC" status. The government takes advantage of those that spend their time making the business prosper and see it result in paying the taxes twice. A "C" corporation that takes the profit it has earned and gives it to the owner has to pay a second income tax on these earnings. If they accumulate cash they can be taxed for not paying themselves a dividend so they are penalized again for financial prudence. Be an "S" or "LLC" in business. You have the protection against personal liability of a corporation but are only taxed once and are not penalized for fiscal responsibility.

## About employees

They made you rich! (Maybe?)
Hire people smarter than you. (Not hard to do)
Motivate them.
Set an example for them.
Talk to them, listen to them.

Sell yourself to them and sell them on the idea they should excel. Make the workplace pleasant. Greet them in the morning and say good night when they leave. Try to know about their family.

Be stern if you detect bullying. I have seen 50 year old ladies gang up on someone they envy.

The best production manager I ever met was a person who managed workers that "feared and loved him."

As a way of making the work place better, when you see an area that needs improving, the best way is to make a visit. Tell them: "I am so pleased that you are never late, that you have a good attitude. We appreciate that. But, your workmanship needs some improvements. Please work on that."

There is a very successful book written by Jack Welsh who did such a magnificent job running GE. I read his books with great interest and admired him very much. However, I totally disagree with his idea that in every group of people you need to increase pay, promote the top ten percent, and let go the bottom ten percent. That last part is cruel and totally disruptive to someone's life. They may be doing the best they can and may need to be moved to a different area and given a chance to do a more menial

task. They do not need to be fired unless they have problems of attitude, work habits or other intolerable problems. They should be fired for cause, but not to remove the
bottom 10 percent. It will give you more profits but that is
not as important as being a good person.

When you build your business you will find some outstanding people—some who do an excellent job in difficult
circumstances. They become your management group.
Everyone could improve and you could make a list of
things that you may wish they would do differently, but if
they are the best, pay them well, motivate them and work
to improve things.

I had an employee that was very likeable. He was in a
remote sales location and was always last in number of
sales. He could be coaxed to change his way but he would
drift back. Should something need to be done quickly and
knowing he was not as busy as the others, we would ask
him to take it on. He would not have time or if he would
accept the project it would take a long time to complete.
When the business went into a decline and it was necessary to reduce the sales staff, he had to be let go. I liked
him a lot but...

Straight commission makes the average person go
from feast to famine. A good year can make them think
good times are forever. Many in the real estate business
are in that feast/famine mode. A decent wage and a bonus
that is tied to something are better for everyone.

You cannot run a big business without people that can
handle sales, accounting, human resources, purchasing,
production, service, research and development. You are as
good as your people. I have had employees that made me

proud. I have had the opposite.

Give them an opportunity. If they indicate a desire to be in sales and you think they do not have the personality for sales, you might be wrong.

I recall a sales person who was successful. He did not have product knowledge. He did not have that personality that would make you enjoy his company. He did not learn or know much about his competitors. He had none of the attributes that you would associate with a good sales person. But he was effective. Someone else had to figure out what he sold but he sold. He would follow up on sales until he had an absolute "no" or he got the sale. I would not want him back, but I think he showed us how being persistent is effective.

Your closest work associates are the people who become your friends. You will attend the weddings and the funerals. You will feel their joy and their sorrows. You, of course, will have friends out of your business but after many years together they will become family. You will cry with them when things go bad.

My personal opinion of the best workers—I include myself also—probably run at 65% efficiency. That can be great if most people are at 45%. There is so much room for improvement of our duties in all of us. We need a life and operating at maximum is not necessary.

## About Buying a Business

First, let me warn you that many business purchases are buying a bad job. If you see a business that you can run that has some advantages over the competition, take a serious look.

I had a friend that wanted to help his son own a business. He purchased a business making brooms. It had a machine that put on the bristles and they sold them to large stores. The units were easy to ship and it was a going business. Its competitors were off shore and had low prices. The buyers were large chains that paid the lowest possible prices. After a few years the business was sold as it had too much competition to be real profitable.

This was buying a job that you had to worry about and be aggressive in marketing. It was manufacturing a commodity. If you sold to a big chain store, they set the price.

Now if a man in poor health with a patent or a unique product that has good profit margins, that would be different. If you bought the business at a reasonable price and ran it well, it could be very successful.

Do not even consider buying a corporation. Buy the assets and start over. You can hire the same people and keep the same name but you do not want any contingent liabilities. Seller gets the same money; you may have an item on your statement called good will. You cannot have your corporation sued by some product failure that you did not even build. I am aware of people purchasing a corporation and being liable for things he never built or owned.

Understand that a corporation is an entity onto itself.

It files a tax return and can have single or multiple owners. In some countries it is called a "limited" because it limits your liabilities. It can fail and so you can lose money, but people owed cannot come back on you personally unless you signed personally.

Be a "Sub S" corporation or state chartered "LLC." A "C" corporation is what the big boys are and they can have thousands of stockholders. A "Sub S" gives you protection from liability but you are taxed as an individual. A "C" corporation pays taxes and you, as the owner, must take funds as dividends and tax is then paid twice. "LLCs" are state formed and treated similar to a "Sub S" but may have different state rules.

It is better to find a *good* job than to purchase an OK job by going into business. You need to find the unique product or method of marketing your product.

Most of the super-rich are the result of public offerings that made them so wealthy and powerful. Our congress by their arrogant ways of making laws with unintended consequences created the Sarbanes Oxley rules on public companies. While I see little benefits, the costs for being a public company have become so expensive that many companies that could have had public offerings, seen great growth and success, have chosen to stay private. Congress continues to stifle business.

Some people lose their job and decide to start a business. That might not be a good idea. The timing could be wrong. Many business opportunities are just buying a bad job. Better to find a new job and keep thinking and keep looking for the wonderful business or new window of opportunity.

There are many business opportunities that are OK. I love radio stations and apartments and farming. They are not great Windows of opportunities with excellent margins but they are good long term investments.

A large, previously quality builder of cell phones is in trouble. They were leaders and built a great phone and did an excellent job of marketing. Their market share is rapidly diminishing. They did not get onto the smart phone quickly and now they see their market share disappear. Some high tech companies are wonderful for a while, but are they going to keep up with the fast changing business.

## Dumb Things I Have Done in Business
### (And smart things I didn't do)

I started remote factories in boom times and then closed them when business went into a slow cycle. I should have just expanded the main manufacturing plant and "eaten the delivery freight" (I was lucky to always sell the property for more than cost) Einstein is supposed to have said "doing the same thing again and again and expecting a different result is being and Idiot." ?? I am kinda guilty.

It is fun to start a new operation, but it's difficult to operate from a distance.

In the window manufacturing business everyone knows who number one is. It is *Anderson Windows*. They operate a factory in Minnesota famous for employee bonus pay. At one time there were three companies building windows that all claimed to our purchasing people that they were number two and most had six or eight factories all over the country. I admired *Anderson* as they were much bigger and had only one location.

When I was a young person building modular homes I noted that I had some competitors that were building panelized homes that were assembled on site. They had a bath core, floor panels, wall panels, ceiling panels, and crews assembled them on site. I had a better way in the modular homes but I thought I should do that also. I did. Why? I do not know. I stopped building the panelized home and improved the modular product I already had, and that was the right thing to do.

My stepfather broke his leg and could not walk. He was in a wheel chair. I purchased a motorized chair and made a ramp for his van. I noticed people had hitch mounted wheel chair carriers on cars and the driver could have the injured get into the car, the driver could run the chair onto the ramp and raise it with a linear actuator and fasten the chair and drive away. The purchased ones were expensive. I built one and it cost around $600 and I thought I should market it at $995 on the internet. I built ten and created the internet web page. Then I thought about it. A house sells often for a lot of money and we are good at it. The corporation could be sued and I did not know anything about the chair lift business. Would it be easier to build one home than sell and service many of this unrelated product? I thought, this would be a good business for someone to start, but it would not fit us. I have given a couple of the chair lifts away and will give away the rest. This would be potentially great little business for someone but not for me.

Today great Iowa and Illinois flat farm land sells from $10,000 per acre to $14,000 per acre. 100 acres can be worth $1,000,000 for farming if it is the best land. It is wonderful collateral for a loan. Did I buy a lot of land for a protection against future inflation? No. Did I realize that we have 7,000,000,000,000 people in the world and you cannot raise corn in the mountains or deserts? Iowa, Illinois, parts of the other Midwestern states will be feeding the world.

Most of us could have bought good farm land for $1000 an acre 15 years ago, as it is excellent collateral for a loan. Most of us did not.

We do have a lot of land that we have accumulated, but most of it is of commercial or residential development type land. When I started a new sales location, I found I could buy 40 acres for not much more than a small commercial plot, and often did.

I have made offers on land and businesses that were not accepted. I thought the price was too high. In hindsight I was wrong, as they increased in value and I should have agreed to a higher price.

As John Wayne once said:

*"Life's tough. It's even tougher if you're stupid."*

## A Production Anomaly

We observed something very interesting in production output. During our period of building mobile homes in the 1970s we had a big back log and were able to sell all we could build. We had a manufacturing building we had built ourselves and it was a modest facility that held the production line. We were able to build two homes a day and we usually worked Saturday to build another so our weekly production was 11 new custom homes. We had a great production supervisor and a really great crew doing everything needed. We had a drafting department, a shipping department, a purchasing department, a quality control department and a sales department.

When we would get a little behind we would add some overtime and maintain our production level. There were five stages of production and we had certain times to make the production line move. We would schedule our sales and all went well.

We, and all of our competitors, were running at full production. As the market seemed to fluctuate according to the Midwest economy, what happened to the rest of the country was not as important as the price of corn in the Midwest.

As you can expect we came to a time when our sales department reported they could not continue to sell in the coming winter at a level of eleven a week, and suggested we make adjustments to reduce the production to seven a week. This seemed the responsible thing to do, so after a meeting we decided to adjust the production level by making a reduction in the assembly line people. We had to have a lay off, and the production supervisor made the choices to reduce the number of production people by about 25%.

The following week we built eleven homes. While all employees are not equal, we had a great group. No one was about to be laid off because of something they did wrong or poorly. The layoff that reduced the number of people did it by the production supervisor reviewing and eliminating the least productive. Those that spent a lot of time visiting with others, that did not seem to work quite as productively were picked. This greatly increased our efficiency but did not solve the problem.

We did not ask the employees to work slower, of course. We did explain that our sales would not allow us to continue to build as many homes so a hopefully short term layoff was necessary.

The next week we added another ten percent people to the layoff. That week we built eleven homes.

The sales staff was worrying about how to get enough orders to keep production going and asked again for more worker layoffs. Again, eleven new homes were built. We did finally have production reduce to match the orders and ran the winter at a level of seven new homes a week.

Spring came and dealer sales increased and optimism reigned. Dealers placed orders and wanted new homes. We were building seven a week and needed an increase to nine homes a week. People were called back to work and the following week we built seven homes. More people were added and we still built seven homes and everyone was busy.

The sales department wanted more homes and people

were added and we finally had production back to the needed eleven.

Why, you ask, did production continue when we wanted it reduced. I do not know. I do know the best were kept and that everyone tried to meet the normal production levels.

Many factories work on production bonus programs and I am sure that works well with a repetitious product. Our homes were quite custom, and were in different sizes and it would have been very difficult to fairly base compensation on production.

I expect a repetitious production of a product might result in ever increasing efficiency.

What lesson was learned? People try to meet expectations and all changes are difficult.

## My China Adventure

We had to travel to sell antennas. I have made several trips to Europe and Scandinavia and a couple to Taiwan. My real adventure, though, was China.

In about 1986 I received a telex from China inquiring about purchasing a spinning machine to make antennas. There was no internet at that time so the international communication was telex. I responded that we had an interest. They responded and asked me to come to China. My response was for them to come to Wisconsin and see us.

We had built a spinning machine for a Company that builds radar detectors. They decided to get into the satellite receiver business and we had agreed to build a machine and operate it with our employees in Henderson, Nevada, adjacent to Las Vegas. This had worked well but when the scrambling came and sales declined, they chose to get out of the business. We brought our machine home.

I forgot about my communications to China until I received another telex saying they were coming, and could I meet them in Madison and make arrangements for them to stay for a week. I agreed and picked them up in Madison and brought them to a hotel in town. I took them to a restaurant that evening and got to know them. Each was unique but all conversation was through the interpreter. None of them had ever been out of their country and the trip through Beijing was the first time they ever were in a big city.

I gave them a tour of operations and invited them to come to my home the next the evening. There were eight people all dressed in identical brown suits. I showed them my farm and farm home. We visited and I answered all of their questions. They became aware that I had a personal airplane and many business interests. It was a pleasant time. They were very impressed.

The next day at a meeting I said I would make an offer. I would take this spinning machine that we had used in Nevada and install a 50 Cycle electric motor to match the Chinese electricity, and ship it to China and sell them one half of it. While I do not recall the exact amount, it was about $130,000 for half. I said I would come over and teach them how to operate it and that I would help them market antennas in Asia; I would get ten percent of the antenna sales for my share. They were very interested.

They also had heard about a store called *Walmart* and wondered if I could take them to a *Walmart* store. I agreed; each of them had a $20 bill to buy personal things. They spent a long time in *Walmart.* They bought many items to bring back to China.

The rest of the time we visited and discussed things, but they wanted me to make a better deal than I had offered. They explained that no one would make the best price first and stick to it. I stayed firm on my price. I took them back to Madison to return to China without a written agreement.

Of the people who came, one was an older gentleman that seemed very kind and considerate. There was also a rather small and unattractive man in the group.

A few months went by and I received a telex that explained that they agreed to my terms and that I should come to Beijing and sign a contract. I agreed and we set a date.

I brought $1000 in cash and my credit cards; I was met in Beijing by the interpreter and taken to a hotel. The next day we had a meeting in a government office. The same group was at the meeting.

In an effort to create some humor in the proceedings, I announced that the smaller gentleman must have gotten away from the group while in Wisconsin, as a local lady said she had met him and went out with him and was pregnant. This brought much laughter and teasing.

Our first discussion was over how much less would I take; I said none, and that I came as they had agreed to my terms. We signed the agreement and they spent time taking me around the city including Tiananmen Square. We went to restaurants and were becoming better friends. When they left, I stayed close to my hotel and only took short walks. I noticed that at that time there were very few cars, but millions of bicycles. The three wheeled bicycles had many sprockets for the chains and they were often hauling more things than a ¾ ton pickup would haul in the US.

Having used my credit cards I returned with my $1000 dollars and we made the changes needed in the machine and arranged shipment.

When the machine arrived in China I received a message that it was there and I and my machine operator should come and "commission" the machine.

We made the arrangement and scheduled the flights and as we got closer to the date, the Tiananmen Square incident came about and the national news covered this event. Some problems arose between our countries and so the trip was delayed.

When some time had passed, they again asked me to come; I suggested there was no need for me coming, and that I felt they were very clever and could figure it out themselves. But they insisted I come. I explained that I did not need to bring an operator, as I could run the machine. They said I would lose face if I worked, and please bring an operator. My nephew was operating spinning machines for me and I asked him to accompany me.

I advised him to pack light as we were going to latitude that was the same as Miami, Florida. I again brought $1000 cash and we left for Beijing, and again we were met by our interpreter. We found with the unrest, credit cards no longer worked, and so I paid cash for airline tickets from Beijing to a city about three hours away in South China. We traveled with the interpreter and upon arrival we were met by a car. The airplane ride was in a Boeing 737 and a pleasant trip. The restroom at the airport was very crude. The ride from the airport to the factory was eight hours in a Toyota.

I drive a ten-year-old pickup when I am in Wisconsin. I do not know if the horn works, as I do not recall ever honking it. We went through many small towns and saw streets filled with bicycles and a few trucks. During our trip, the horn blasted a thousand times. We would come over a rise and be able to see 50 miles and I could almost not comprehend the view of a 1000 small farms with people with very primitive agricultural equipment. Sometimes I could see a machine with a small gas engine, but farming was done mostly with oxen and horses. The population was very dense and we were in the mountains.

I was told that during the Second World War the Japanese quickly over ran Shanghai and the government thought industry should be in the mountains.

It was a high altitude and I was cold. I was given a coat much like the picture of the Korean War Chinese soldiers.

We were taken to a place to stay at night. It was two rooms in a nearby small town and next to a river. We were picked up in the morning and brought to the satellite complex and ate together in the evening.

The first question was "how is the baby?" I of course reported a beautiful healthy baby and the accused father was acting proud.

The facility was over staffed by 300 percent. They made their own bolts in a lathe and had caves dug in the mountain in which to put their equipment in case of war. The facility was perhaps 25 acres and protected by a high stone wall.

The machine worked well, the company was great, and each evening as we ate together, we became closer friends. I had brought gifts for each. We ate at a table that could rotate with many things to eat. Often a drink was poured, a toast was made and it was a good time.

We operated the new machine with about 50 people watching and soon they were able to operate it also.

I took a few walks in the complex and noted people sweeping the streets and seemingly not too busy.

When it came time to leave, each of them shook my hand and made a statement that was interpreted to me. The older gentleman refused to take my hand but instead gave me a big hug. They are neat people and very much like us.

This was in 1987, so of course their world has changed considerably. I had long talks with the lady interpreter who, along with her husband, had college educations. She asked many questions about the US and was very careful not to say anything against the government. They had been taken from College during the time of the power of the Red Guard and made to work in rice paddies. She had two sons and a home with bicycles and a TV set. She said she had no hope of ownership of an automobile but that things were better than they had been.

The factory made antennas prior to our arrival and

they had been in sections and they wanted the better spun aluminum ones.

Today you can email China and ask for a quote and get an instant low price without any dealing. At that time they thought everything should be discussed for a long time and prices argued about.

As we did a lot of business in Australia we soon had a request for a quote for antennas that could be made by that machine. I telexed them and their quote was higher than if we had built them and shipped from The US. I told them that they were too high and they said 'What would they pay?" We were not successful in our program of helping them market them. We still own one half of a machine in China. Fortunately I charged enough for half of the machine so we did okay.

When I returned to Wisconsin I did not have enough cash left from the money I had taken with me to pay the fee at the airport for my car, and I had to have my brother meet me to pay the bill.

## When a Good Business Goes Bad

In 1972 while our modular home company was growing and being successful, we saw big growth in the mobile home industry. Because of the lobbying of the mobile home industry, states changed their laws on over width movement; mobile home builders began making them wider and longer. Because each state law was different, some states allowed wider and longer units than others. As I watched this industry I felt I should market a mobile home also. I looked at them all and looked at the pricing. They were all sold to dealers, and many were built very cheaply and were not a good value. An automobile has a window price which gives the buyer some idea of what they are worth. The mobile home dealer could mark it up as much as he wished that day.

The industry was selling the product to people often for temporary housing and for this they were a good value. A young farmer may plan to take over the farm in a few years and so they would buy the trailer to live in until the parents retired.

Trailer parks were developed and financing was created for mobile homes. The interest rates were very high and the buyers were often not sophisticated. The mobile home was personal property and so it would depreciate in value with its value being determined by its age and size.

The industry grew rapidly in the early 1970s and as I watched it grow I felt there was an opportunity for an upscale and better unit.

I built a prototype and put it on display and contacted

dealers to see if I could sell them one. I would call a dealer and tell them I would like to pick them up in our airplane and show the home. They would bring a friend for an airplane ride to our factory and look it over. They were polite but did not want to buy it. Again I had thought I was a good designer and I was not.

I looked at everything that others built and while not nearly as good as ours, they were much sharper looking. They had furniture and decorator items and while cheaply constructed, they were very attractive.

I, being the optimistic, had been constructing a factory for building mobile homes. So I took one of the most popular selling plans of a competitor and made mine very similar. They used 2" x 2" sidewalls studs and I used 2" x 4" with more insulation. I had an attractive vaulted ceiling and a step up dining area. My home had regular residential doors and looked good.

I took this new 14' x 68' mobile home to a trade show and dealers placed many orders. I was a bit embarrassed when the sales manager of the unit I had copied stopped and looked at it. As he was leaving he said "you missed something... we had a small statue in the living room decorations."

We were on our way to setting up dealers who became friends. We built a big back order file and added floor plans and options. While our homes sold for more, they also cost more. We were profitable but without a big return on sales. It was a fun business and the dealers were nice people and making a lot of money.

During the time from the early 1960s until the late 1980s mobile homes grew to be more than 25 percent of all new homes built.

The dealers were buying from many different manu-facturers and so there was competition for the product. The economy went in cycles and so did the industry. We always felt we should keep our employees working all year so our company has always built inventory in the winter to sell in the summer. This works well if you have the money and orders to carry you into early winter.

Some of the manufacturers came up with a bonus pro-gram for a dealer. If you purchased $1,000,000 worth you could receive a rebate of 1% or $10,000. If you would go beyond this number you could get retroactive increases and this could grow to 5%.

Dealers who ordered homes from us would often want to cancel the order when fall came to order something else with a bigger bonus.

When inflation came (Jimmy Carter era, big inflation and 20% prime rate) we would find that having a big back order would mean when we did build the home, material costs had increased and it cost us more than we expected.

We also found that our competitors were setting our selling price as they would make package deals with which we had to compete.

We found the dealers (our friends) who would often not treat the customers well and did not set up the unit properly. We would get complaints. We found that dealers often did not have good financial sense and so would not be able to pay us as agreed. Sometimes we would find a dealer that would bill us for repairing roof leaks and he claimed 10 of the 12 he purchased had leaks he repaired while another dealer that sold 24 never had a single leak.

Some dealers were not honest with us or their customer.

As I thought about this I realized that we had a great business in the modular homes sold factory direct, and not so good a business in building the mobile homes. We could use that factory and resources for our primary business.

In the summer of 1988 I sent a letter to all of the 50 plus North American Mobile home dealers that we were going to stop production in January of the year 1990. During the last 3 months of 1990 we were very busy filing orders for new North Americans.

Many of those dealers remained friends and stayed in the business. A couple of things happened to this business. Some financial companies created finance units that would finance a very high percentage of the cost. They would borrow money to finance them and when an economic down turn came the finance companies went broke. This caused an overreaction by the normal banks that became afraid to finance them. The industry went into a decline that made them become less than one percent of new homes today.

As that business went into a decline, many mobile home builders began to build modular homes and sell them to dealers. When the housing market went into the deep decline of 2007 many of the manufacturers went broke and the dealers failed or stopped business.

During our largest year of production we built 700 new custom homes. Today, when we profitably build one third of that amount, in our market we are the big builder. At our lower production rates we are still profitable because we are debt free and have cash in the bank. Had we always been expanding to the extent of our available credit, we would have had great difficulty in the housing decline. I am glad we chose to be careful and work to achieve being debt free and have money in the bank.

Our 18 years of building the North American manufactured home was, over all, profitable and an Ok business.

## Delta Hotel Aviation

Airplanes are great. In business they can make a productive person more productive. During the early years
with many sales locations I could come to work, spend two
hours handling problems, take a walk through the factories
and then go to the airport and fly to a sales location. They
all were placed so there was easy access to an airport. I
would do a walk-around of the display, making lists of
things I would suggest, talking about any problems and
then going back to the airport for a trip to another location,
and on to a third or fourth. This allowed me to accomplish
much in one day and still keep myself up to date on the
things happening in the corporate office.

A problem with airplanes is that smaller, older aircraft
flown by pilots that are not professionals are statistically
more dangerous than driving a car. Weather is always a
concern and you can improve the statistics if you are cau-
tious about weather, do not ever drink and fly, and try to
keep current in your flying. Another problem is that they
are expensive to own and operate, and you *can* get along
without them.

As our company grew we reached a point that we
could justify a larger airplane and that we could justify two
pilots on some trips. We chose to have a professional pilot
that also had other duties. Reviewing the costs, I realized
that the best solution was to place the large aircraft on a
lease to an aircraft FBO (fixed base operator) that did charter flying. By sharing the revenue we could have an aircraft
available for company use and generate some income from

this use. We chose to form a separate corporation and have been pleased with the result. Our Citation often flies charter trips with famous people, large corporation executives and politicians. Our aircraft business does generate income and makes the aircraft available for company use.

1942 L3 defender that helped win WW 2 N48015

Our oldest of the three airplanes is an Aronca L3 Defender that was in the Second World War. I enjoy giving rides and flying this wonderful antique. When the Second World War started all airplane companies were converted to build airplanes for the war effort. The L2 was the Taylor craft, the L3 was the Aronca, L4 was the Piper and the L5 was the Stinson. Each was modified for its special use with the Stinson used as an ambulance airplane. It had an interior place for and injured person and a rack on the wing strut for another. The L3 was for artillery observation and its modifications were more Plexiglas for better visibility and a handle so door hinge pins could be removed, so the door would fall off and you could jump out if needed. The L3 is used to give rides often to WW 2 veterans. I received a call from a friend that had told a retired National Guard General about it and he had flown one in the war. I rode along while he took it for a ride.

Granddaughter Amber performing pre-flight
inspection of the Seneca N444DH

Our work horse airplane is the Seneca II. It is a turbo-charged twin engine airplane that can carry 6 people and can fly about 800 miles at about 200 miles per hour. It is not a sports car, but more like a hard working van. Because it is turbocharged it can fly much higher and it has an oxygen system which is rarely used but does allow us to go higher when the tail winds are good.

We also have a Citation CJ2 Jet that is certified to fly up to 45 thousand feet and one that can go nonstop to any place in the US from Wisconsin. Most airline flights are in the 35 thousand feet area, and being able to climb higher lets us have less headwinds going West, and sometimes coming East we can pick the altitude that has the best tailwind. The air temperature is lower at higher altitudes so it is more efficient at the highest altitudes. It can carry nine people and goes almost 500 Miles per hour. I have taken the training and I am type rated to fly the airplane.

Citation N475DH

HOW TO GET RICH SLOW

## Marcella Farquar?

Marcella did not exist. She was a made up person.

During our early years there were times we needed to respond to a request. Sometimes this response was not something pleasant to do. As an example a home purchaser would write a letter asking for their new home to be put on the schedule ahead of the other customers for some reason they thought important. We could not do that as others were also waiting for a new home and it would be unfair. We would need to respond so we would write the letter and sign it Marcella Farquar.

Soon other people in the company would use her name. We would put Marcella's name on the schedule, and if we got behind (As the schedule often would) we could just remove her name and be back on schedule.

We would get a request for us to do something that was not part of our responsibility, such as back fill the customer's yard. Our contract did not include that. Marcella would respond and explain why it could not be done.

Our models had no storm door and we did not show them on models or include them with a new home, as they were often damaged while the people were moving in and we would be replacing them. When someone would contact us and ask where the storm door was, Marcella would respond.

When a phone call came for Marcella, we honestly said "she is not in today."

If we wanted information about a product but not be bothered by sales people, it was Marcella who made the inquiry.

If we wanted a brochure from a competitor it was Marcella who would call and ask for it.

Marcella received a lot of mail after a while.

The impression we had of our fictional girl was she drove a Harley but had no tattoos and did not allow bad language.

## Fun projects to work on
## (But with no prospects of profits)

We all need recreation. Without interests other than work your life is incomplete. We all have interests that are unique to us. While I like many things such as golf and flying, my lifelong interest has been automobiles. I started collecting with the purchase of a 1927 model T ford coupe almost 50 years ago. I paid $250 for it and have enjoyed it. One time in the early 1960s my Oldsmobile would not start because of the cold weather. I went to my model T, primed it, cranked it, and drove it to work.

My brother had owned it and modified it only to have more choices of gears. A model T Ford had twenty horse power and a two speed transmission. Ford sold cars without a body so people could make bread trucks, milk trucks and other work vehicles. They also offered a Ruxtal two speed rear end to give more power and then twice as many gears. My brother installed a Ruxtal, which gave my car a total of 4 speeds ahead.

Another (accessory shop) option was a Warford three speed transmission for fords that was installed behind the regular transmission. He installed it so my model T now has a total of 13 speeds ahead. (2 times 2, times 3 plus two reverse gears which is another forward gear. Reverse, low and reverse means it goes forwards very, very slowly.)

I put up a building on my farm for a shop and cars. I guess I want the cars for something to work on. I do NOT collect perfectly wonderful cars and store them. I want to improve them and make them better, so most of my cars were really rough and in need of work. The model T Speedsters did not really exist, as I started with a frame and built them from parts.

My next vehicle was a 1938 Ward La France fire truck. Our town had an annual event called the "Great Fire Engine Race" A few collectors and local fire departments had a fun day of driving around to small towns (not at all racing) and have events like putting up a ladder and climbing up to put a beer can on a pole. It was a timed event. Silly but fun. The Ward La France Company heard about it and funded publicity, and soon it was a very large event. I was on the committee and met with the sponsor who said a great truck was available from the Manhasset/Lakeville fire department near New York City. It is a very long truck with ladders. I bought it and brought it back as my fire truck. I installed a beer tap in the side and collected a crew to ride along.

For a few years it was a fun, successful event and Charles Karult from CBS "On the road" came to cover it along with many TV stations. A few years later an accident with a serious injury happened and the event stopped. My fire truck runs great and gets an annual run. Because it is over 70 years old it can be excused for sounding its siren without an emergency.

When my son married, he asked if the fire truck could pick up the wedding party from the church and run through town with the siren sounding, and of course I agreed. It went to the reception and was the source of tap beer.

Ambers wedding party

Years later, my daughter was married and of course the fire truck was the vehicle that brought the wedding party from the church to the reception and the source of beer. When my granddaughter was married, she asked her dad if they could use the fire truck and he said NO, that it was too far to bring it to the wedding. Of course, Amber asked grandpa, and the fire truck continued the family tradition.

When a new bridge was built from Iowa to our town on the Mississippi, the mayor asked if the truck could haul the city council and friends as the first vehicle to cross the bridge. I agreed and found that 50 people can ride a ladder truck. My collection was now two vehicles.

In about 1970 the local Cadillac dealer had a 1946 Willys Jeep for a snow plow vehicle. I asked to buy it and he said no. He said he needed it. I continued to ask to buy it and finally he sold it to me. It was identical to the World War II Jeeps. I made a roll bar and it became a family favorite, painted red, and was fun to drive around the farm. I paid $250 for it and it came with a snow plow that I sold for $250. My basic cost was then nothing. As this was identical to an Army Jeep, I painted it military and have since added a dummy machine gun. My car collection became three.

I found a Model A Ford roadster and bought it. It looked pretty bad and did not run. I brought it home and installed a battery and tried to start it. It did not start. I checked the ignition system which is unique to Model A Fords and made sure the spark plugs fired and that the timing was correct. I checked the gas and the gas was in the carburetor so it should have run but it did not. I was really surprised and decided to remove the cylinder head and found that through the many years the valves were stuck and one was totally burned. I bought one new valve and lubricated the others and after putting it together had a nice car.

The color of Fords were 100 percent black up to 1928, and then *most* of them were black. I read that a short run of 20 Model As were made red, so I painted it red. It is a great fun vehicle as it has a rumble seat. My car collection was four.

I found a 1951 Ford convertible for sale and purchased it. The car had been owned by kids and while it was mechanically excellent it had been treated without much care and needed a big cleaning and a paint job. A great fun car. My car collection was five.

A nurse in our town retired and had a 1954 Ford Victoria. It is a great car that has been driven carefully. It was a new model that was called a hard top convertible. While not a convertible it had no door post. I had it repainted and now my collection was six.

I used to drive by a business that had a Model A truck chassis parked by a warehouse. I inquired about buying it and then I had another collectable car. Its body was falling apart and really not something to save. I knew that trolleys were made using trucks, so I started to build a trolley that could hold about 15 people. It was mostly wood work, but it worked out well. The only problem was everyone that knew about it wanted it to be the wedding car. The collection was now seven.

A local dealer traded in a 1971 Ford convertible that ran great. I purchased it, had it painted and added it to the collection, and now the collection was eight.

I heard about a 1948 Ford coupe that was for sale and I bought it. It is now a sharp and great car. My collection was now nine.

I learned of a very low mileage Mercedes convertible that I thought was beautiful and so I purchased it. It's black and has both a hard top and a soft top. The collection became ten cars.

I added a Jaguar convertible to the collection. It is a 1999 and while not too old, it is collectable and fun to drive. My collection became eleven.

My collector car number twelve is a longer story. Henry Ford has always been my hero. He started the *Ford Motor Car Company* that exists to this day. The car was designed to be simple and for the masses. Henry Ford's best friend was Thomas Edison. They took vacations together and owned adjacent houses in Ft Meyers, Florida.

When the new Ford Company was started there were more electric cars then gas cars in the country. Edison told

Ford in 1909 that he should make the new model T gasoline powered and with so low a compression that it would run on kerosene. There was more kerosene than gas in rural America. He said there was no electricity in rural America and so the model T should not be electric. It did come with instructions on making Ethanol/Whiskey. The model T had a magneto and so there was no battery. The cowl lights and the tail lights were kerosene and were adequate in rural areas. They also had Acetylene lights. There was a small tank on the running board that held water and when you wanted brighter lights you turned on water to drip on carbide and acetylene gas would form. It would go up a pipe to the head lights that you would light with a match. They were much brighter than kerosene lights.

Ford prospered and soon became the biggest car company in the world. In fact, he made more cars than all the rest combined. The cars were often sold without a body so it could be a milk truck or a specialty vehicle. Hundreds of thousands were shipped all over the world.

In 1915 Edison invented a nickel based battery. It was Thomas Edison's 1051st patent. This is the NICAD battery used in the hybrids such as the *Prius*. It was lighter and held a bigger charge; Edison told Ford he should build an electric car with this new battery. Edison said ladies do not want to crank a car and it is silent. At that time the biggest maker of electric cars was Baker in Cleveland. Ford decided to build some prototype electric Fords. After building the prototypes, Henry Ford announced they would offer an electric car, but they never did put it into production.

Also at that time some people did not just want another model T Ford. They wanted a car with more style so they would buy a model T chassis and build a Ford Speedster. There were thousands of speedsters built by many people, so all were a bit different, but also similar. Most had the monocle windshield. Often they were raced. Many were modified with more power, so the 20 HP engine would be hopped up to 25 or 30HP.

I had been building a model T Speedster from parts. As I would move in the fall to Florida, I was going from being very busy, to having a lot of free time. I put together a speedster in Florida and had it complete except for the engine. I made the fenders and body and enjoyed the project. As I returned for the summer, I had plans to overhaul the engine and install it in the fall. Then I read about the Ford electrics and decided to make it electric.

I bought an electric motor, batteries and a controller and I now have a 97 year old model T that is similar to the Ford Electric prototype. It goes 25 mph; it goes 20 miles on a charge and is fun to drive on back streets. I did something that Ford and Edison could not do. I installed two solar panels to charge the batteries and to extend its range. I could use a charger but I do not. I let it sit in the sun until full charged and then go for a ride. My car collection became twelve cars.

1916 Model T ford Speedster electric with solar panels

With my Electric model T completed I felt I needed another similar project; I decided to build another model T Speedster. While in Florida I can golf three days a week. I can be on the internet and phone for business, but I do have a lot of free time. I found a frame and engine from a 1913 model T and a better engine from a parade car. I have a small shop, and so I made the fenders and splash pans, the wooden body, and completed anther speedster.

While I have never attended a model T Ford Speedster race, they were very popular and were often raced at county fairs. I recall seeing model T Speedsters being worked on prior to a race. I wish I had been able to attend such a race. The engine was 20 HP and the ignition system was four separate buzzer coils that made it easy to start but not run at high RPM. My Collection is now thirteen.

1913 Model T Speedster

I would not sell any of the collected cars even if offered much more than they are worth. I would also not buy a perfect car and store it as my enjoyment is working on them. It is a hobby, and everyone has a special interest. Our life is more complete and enjoyable if we do those things we enjoy. If you enjoy horses, raise them. We need interests other than our work.

## My Railroad Adventures

My farm is 105 acres on the bank of the Wisconsin River about four miles from the Mississippi. The railroad tracks were built from Milwaukee to the Mississippi river in about 1850. They put temporary tracks on the ice in the winter and in the summer used ferry boats to bring rail cars across the Mississippi river.

In the 1970s the rail line on my farm belonged to the Milwaukee Road. They stopped running rail cars on the tracks as they were in financial trouble. The railroad tracks grew up in weeds.

I had a friend who came upon a set of four wheels that had been on a small rail car. These were not large and probably were from a work flat car pulled behind a small work car. He commented it would be fun to make a small car to run on the railroad tracks. I had a riding lawn mower that was about wore out, and so together we made a frame, mounted the wheels and bolted on the mower engine and had a railroad motor car. It was belt driven but it worked. We took along a dog and a beer cooler and went down the tracks. While it was great fun it seemed the dog enjoyed it the most. The problem was the belt would get tangled up in the weeds and so we decided it was unsatisfactory. As it was my motor and his wheels it was our rail car. He decided to buy a 5 HP motor with a centrifugal clutch and a chain to have a better vehicle. It was then his rail car.

I found someone that owned a small flat rail car that was pulled behind a work rail car used by work crews; I bought it. I found an 8 HP motor and bought a clutch, two sprockets and a chain, and then we had two rail cars.

Every time we took a trip we brought along the dog and it really was fun. We had to go East, and we soon came upon large bridges crossing the river. The tracks were often on islands so we would see much wildlife. We would usually run the two of our motor cars together, and each trip, we'd go a bit further. There happened to be a bar in each small town, and soon we had many people that wanted to go for the train ride.

One day while at work I received a call from the front desk saying there were two railroad detectives that wanted to see me. As people often joked about the train rides I thought she was joking and said, "Send them in, smarty."

I then met two really big guys who had credentials that showed they were employees of the Milwaukee Railroad. They sat down and stated: "We have heard that you have a homemade railroad motor car and have been trespassing on our railroad. Is that true?" My response was, "No, that is not true, but I will quit if you want." They were nice guys and we agreed I had not done it, but that I had agreed to quit. Soooo... I quit.

A couple of years later the Milwaukee Railroad went into bankruptcy and the property was sold to the state of Wisconsin. While I had made a deal with the Milwaukee Railroad, *I had no deal with Wisconsin.*

I had met a person who had a real railroad motor car for sale. It was a Fairmont that had a 22 HP *Onan* engine with an electric starter. It had a transmission that would allow it to run as well in either direction, so it did not need to be turned around. I was back in the rail business. I converted the old unit back to just a flat car to pull with some lawn chairs and was soon giving rides again.

One winter day a group of friends and I were talking about the fun of running the car and someone suggested we set a day for a trip east. We decided that we would go east until we were arrested. The group decided that it should be the last Sunday in June. We decided we would leave very early and just go. As the word spread, a friend received a phone call from a gentleman that was a college professor in Missouri, but who was a rail buff. I had known his father who was an elderly gentleman and chairman of the board of the bank where I was a director. He wanted to ride along and we agreed. A doctor was part of the group and as the time came closer we had a meeting. It was suggested that our original plan of a very early start was silly. As one of the group was an excellent cook, it was decided we would take a grill and stop for breakfast on the big trestle crossing the river near Woodman, Wisconsin.

New people joined our group and a few decided not to go, but our Sunday came with a beautiful day. The farthest we had ever gone before was about 30 miles to Boscobel, Wisconsin. We left on the motor car pulling the flat car and started up the river. We arrived at the Bridge at Woodman about 9 AM with the temperature climbing up to about 80 degrees. We sat on the trestle and had this big breakfast while canoes were going under the bridge. The Wisconsin River is fast moving but a wonderful river for canoeing (and railroading). There are sand bars all over. We had a great breakfast while greeting the people going down river.

When we came to Boscobel we had to cross a main highway. As trains had not been on the tracks for several years the street had been blacktopped and the tracks did not exist. We had to push and steer onto the tracks at the other side, and soon we were heading east out of Boscobel. We came to a siding and the cars became derailed because a switch had been thrown. Everyone had to take a picture. We soon had the train back on the track and were heading into new country. We came upon a fence crossing the track. A farmer had put it up to allow his cattle on each side of the tracks. We took it down to cross and then put it back up.

We stopped at Muscoda as someone wanted to stop in a tavern. When he did not return, another went to get him; soon more went for the first two and it was a while before the crew was back on the motor car.

We soon came upon another big trestle crossing the river as we came near Lone Rock, Wisconsin. As we continued we came to an area by a field that was being irrigated; as it was very warm, the water spray was welcome. The next town was Spring Green, Wisconsin. The tracks ran right through town.

Should you ever be in Wisconsin on the last Sunday in June, go to Spring Green. There is an annual celebration event with the town full of people. We were not aware of that.

As we came to the center of town the high school band was set up near the tracks and was playing. What a welcome!

We spent a long time in Spring Green and soon the crews were separated into several different taverns. We finally assembled the crew and headed East towards Madison and our goal of getting into trouble.

Another beautiful, large bridge showed up and we were very hot. We stopped our motor car and all went down to the river to swim a bit and to lie on a sand bar.

Back in the motor car we continued toward Madison. We came to Mazomanie; someone wisely suggested that maybe we should return to Spring Green and call for a ride home.

Our doctor friend had a large van and so he called his wife, we placed the motor car off the tracks and returned home, tired. A crew from our company went the next day with a trailer and brought the motor car back.

Later, as the state owned the tracks, they made arrangements for each county to fix up their portion so the tracks could be leased out to a short line operator. I received a phone call from the supervisor of the Iowa county department of highways. He asked if it was correct that I had a railroad motor car and would I rent it? I said sure. They picked it up and used it for a few months. The used motor car was not excellent. It worked but was not great. The County truck came one day and brought it back. Their mechanics had gone through it and made everything excellent. New battery, everything cleaned up and working perfect. The last week of the year I received a letter and $100 for rent of my motor car. That was a good deal for me. Soon the State had leased the tracks to a short line operator.

I parked the motor car on my land near the tracks so we could easily get on the tracks and go for an evening ride. We could check on when the last train came and when the next one would come. I agreed with a hunting group that I would take them for a ride and one evening we all took the tractor and wagon and went down to the tracks. We checked first that no train was coming. The motor car was gone. We had to cancel that trip and so I went to the airport and took the L3 Defender for an inspection of the tracks to see if I could find it abandoned. I flew at about 35 miles an hour and 300 feet, but I could find no trace of the motor car.

The tracks were being used by a short rail line in Janesville, Wisconsin so I called them and told them that my motor car that had been parked on my land was taken. I asked did you take it? A returned call said their crews saw it and took it. We went to Janesville with a pickup and a trailer and brought it back.

This was not the last motor car trip. The tracks are now in use and trains haul freight to Prairie du Chien. Usually the people who unload know when they are coming and when they go back. We do not go anymore (sure??)

## Random thoughts

Our free enterprise system is the reason this country is great and a wonderful place for business. We should forever be grateful to our founding fathers that made this possible.

We need some rules and they come at us with great speed. When I built my first home, few codes existed. I could have built it any way I wanted. Good builders wanted a good reputation and so they built well. Some bad builders caused the beginning of codes. No one can object to codes for health and safety. There are good reasons for codes for energy efficiency and safety. The problems become too many codes.

My first house floor plan was silly. The living room too big, bedrooms to small, too much hall, and just dumb. While the house was strong it did not have great workmanship. When I sold it the buyer purchased it at a great price because an amateur built it. The buyer received a great value of a very low priced new home.

Who could fault OSHA? They have implemented rules that have saved lives and avoided injury. They hired an army of inspectors and every year it implements many rules that are extreme and silly, and they found that fines are a source of income. I and most people would feel safe to climb a ladder that extended a bit above the roof. The ladder must extend 36 inches and if it is 30 you are in violation and are fined. I am glad there is OSHA; I just wish they made us a lot safer and then quit with new rules. They will not, it is a revenue source.

In Wisconsin I have a farm and I can plow up any area I want. If I build a commercial building, I need an "erosion control permit." This requires us to pay an engineer to design it with silt fence and some other things. There is a fee. The original permit was a small fee and for a larger area. Now it is much smaller area (to require more fee generating permits) and is a state income source. I built a golf course. I filled out the erosion control information and it was approved. When I built a hotel and banquet facility, I was told I needed an engineer to submit it. I hired the engineer, wrote the check and mailed it and knew I had to wait to excavate it. I dug a hole to see if I would hit rock and the erosion control police drove by, saw my small hole and we were in trouble. The fine that resulted was paid and it was put into the newspaper. When government says "We are here to help you" and you say "welcome," two liars have met.

When I had built my first house I thought if I could build 10 homes really inexpensive and rent them, I could live my life without working. Just collect rent and vacation all the time. Nice day dream, but not something you would do if you *had* accomplished it.

My grandson argued with Grandpa. "Grandpa I love to play Black Jack at a casino and that is gambling, but you invest in the stock market and that is gambling, too." Of course, I respond "There is a difference between investing and gambling." I have owned Oracle stock for many years; I invested $10,000 and now I have about $80,000 and no income tax paid. I have gifted some of this stock to charities and have taken a deduction. Buy quality and hold, buy quality when you want to invest and do not be concerned about timing. Stocks go up and go down but quality, over time, grows tax free. I also told Billy "if you are a really good poker player and want to play with your friends, and the house does not take a cut, that is much different than going to Las Vegas and playing." If you play the roulette table and they only take 6% and you play 20 minutes to run your hundred dollars through, and stay there four hours you are statistically broke. If everyone that gambled would say I will play and take my $100 and quit when I win $100, and I will agree to lose $300 before I quit, the casinos would not make much money. They would still generate money but much less. A graph of your status would show you going up and going down and people have a limit on what they will lose, but not on how much they win.

Inflation is always going to exist. It may be slow and sometime there may be deflation for a while but over time, cash becomes worth less and stuff becomes worth more. I bought some *Krugerands* once for $500. Today they are worth $1800 each. I built apartments that cost about $15,000 a unit to build. Over 30 years they have created income each year and today are worth double that even being old but well maintained. Land, income producing buildings are great hedges against the inevitable inflation. What is the lowest price? A new black and white 17 inch TV cost over $400 in 1955 and many working people were making $2000 a year. The similar tube type before digital came along was under $100. We bought a plastic skylight for some years. It was three parts and we paid $120 for them. They became popular and we were pleased when they went under $100 and then a major window company started offering a better one for $40. I do not know what a lowest price is of anything.

As I write this the housing market is not great. We are running at a rate much less than the best year, but we are still profitable. MOST of our competitors are gone. They are either bankrupt or just out of business because of high debt loads. Could we have survived a big down turn in housing in 2007 with high debt? No. Business is fun. I love to come to work and make sales and develop new products and have things happen. Sometimes a truck is broken down and people are angry that things did not happen. You need to solve those problems that are not fun to enjoy the fun stuff. New projects are fun. The most profitable thing is to do more of that which works and that is okay, but not usually as much fun.

The world changed once the post office was a job for life. The internet has changed that and continues to change it. The business of steady growth is in decline. Many industries that have been around forever and all of a sudden you see change. How many car insurance companies on TV can save you $500? When I discuss our future with our managers I encourage them to change things to be better, as we do not want to become another *Kodak!* Change for good is wonderful. Change for change sake is stupid. Why did GM come up with a funny battery with a side post years ago. It was a problem as it was different—and not better. GM owners had to buy something special and it was difficult to put on booster cables. It was dumb. That was not the cause of them going broke; it was doing many dumb things that caused GM to go bankrupt.

*Drive your business or it will drive you.* Ben Franklin

**Things to avoid**:

Debt! Necessary but pay it off as soon as possible.

Promises you cannot keep.

Bad work habits setting bad examples to employees.

Arrogance. We owe courtesy to everyone.

Drinking so it has an effect on your work.

Smoking.

Foolish spending. Build a cash reserve, plan for the worst.

Not being productive every day.

*Pleasure in the job puts perfection in your work.*
Aristotle 384 BC

## My choices of some great people from the last 100 years who have changed the world with some of their very interesting quotations

**Henry Ford**: He maybe had the biggest impact on our country in the last century. He loved to tinker and take things apart. He became good at repairing watches. He Married Clara in 1888 and moved to Detroit in 1891. He became an apprentice and after the apprenticeship he became certified machinist. In 1895 he constructed a horseless carriage with electrical ignition that he developed.

Ford started production of the model T Ford in late 1908 and it became a success. While being credited with the assembly line, he did not develop it but perfected one in 1913. Ford felt he should share profits and so during a period in which he could have hired workers for much less, he chose to pay $5 per day. He continued to lower the price and increase the quality of the car.

The Model T was the bestselling car in the world and by the early 1920s was larger than all the other car companies in the world. More than 15,000,000 Model T cars were sold and in the 1920s a new model T Ford could be purchased for $260. During the Second World War his Willow Run plant built most of the 18,000 B-24 aircraft along with jeeps, and tanks.

*"Chop your own wood and it will warm you twice"*

*"When everything seems to be going against you, remember that the airplane takes off against the wind, not with*
*it ...."*

*"You say I started out with practically nothing, but that isn't correct. We all start with all there is, it's how we use it that makes things possible."*

*"Coming together is the beginning. Keeping together is progress. Working together is success."*

*"One of the greatest discoveries a person makes, one of their great surprises, is to find they can do what they were afraid they couldn't do."*

*"Vision without execution is just hallucination."*

*"Quality means doing it right when no one is looking."*

**Thomas Edison**: Probably the most prolific inventor of all of time, he was four years of age before he learned to talk and was described by teachers as a difficult student. He had a total of 1093 patents and his 1051st was the nickel based, lighter NICAD battery. He died in 1931 at 84 years of age. He was enthusiastic about Lincoln and made posters for his campaigns.

While revered by presidents and while he accomplished much, he made a poor choice in arguing for DC electricity rather than AC. Tesla correctly argued for AC which could be transformed to higher or lower frequencies and travel great distances with less loss. Edison felt AC was dangerous, and of course, history showed him wrong. (Tesla was right but died poor)

He came from poverty to wealth and was an early investor in GE. GE today is the only company left as part of the original Dow Jones industrial average.

Some of his many quotations:

*"My main purpose in life is to make enough money to create ever more inventions."*

*"Genius is one percent inspiration, and ninety nine percent perspiration."*

*"Opportunity is missed by most people because it is dressed in overalls and looks like work."*

*"The first requisite for success is to develop the ability to focus and apply your mental and physical energies to the problem at hand without growing weary."*

*"Inspiration can be found in a pile of junk. Sometimes you can put it together and with good imagination and invent something."*

*"I enjoy working 18 hours a day. Besides the short catnaps I take each day I average about 4 or 5 hours of sleep per night."*

*"If we all did the things we are really capable of doing, we would literally astound ourselves."*

*"I have more respect for the person with a single idea who gets there than for a person with a thousand ideas and accomplishes none."*

*"Many of life's failures are experienced by people who did not realize how close they were to success when they gave up."*

*"Surprises and reverses can serve as an incentive for great accomplishment. There are no rules here; we are just trying to accomplish something."*

*"As a cure for worrying, work is far better than whiskey."*

*"The only time I become discouraged is when I think of all the things I would like to do and the little time I have in which to do them."*

*"The thing I lose patience with the most is the clock. Its hands move too fast."*

*"Time is really the only capital that any human being has and the one thing he can least afford to waste or lose."*

*"Someday, man will harness the rise and fall of the tides, imprison the power of the sun and release atomic power."*

*"It is obvious that we don't know one millionth of one*

*percent about anything."*

*"I believe that the science of chemistry alone almost proves the existence of an intelligent creator."*

*"If parents pass enthusiasm along to their children, they will leave them an estate of incalculable value."*

**Steve Jobs:** History will look at his accomplishment and will remember him in the way they remember Thomas Edison. His biography shows the real Jobs. It shows a strange person who felt his adventures with LSD made him a better person. His products gave the company the ability to accumulate 100 billion in cash. His history showed a flawed person who in spite of his 80% wrong moves was vindicated by the 20% that were truly wonderful. He started with nothing, became rich and changed the world.

He agonized over the color of the yellow in the logo of the NEXT computer for weeks, holding everything up. Was that good? No. Was his dedicated concern to push the people to make things of the best quality? Yes. Was his unwarranted vulgar public degrading a good employee? No. Was pushing his employees to the extreme successful? Yes.

Quotations of Steve Jobs:

*"Market research is of no value as customers do not know what they want until you show them."*

*"Being the richest man in the cemetery doesn't matter to me. Going to bed at night saying we've done something wonderful, that's what matters to me."*

*"But Apple really beats to a different drummer. I used to say that Apple should be the Sony of this business, but in reality, I think Apple should be the Apple of this business. But innovation comes from people meeting up in the hallways or calling each other at 10:30 at night with a new idea, or because they realized something that shoots holes in how we've been thinking about a problem. Computers themselves, and software yet to be developed, will revolutionize the way we learn. Design is a funny word. Some people think design means how it looks. But of course, if you dig deeper, it's really how it works. Each year has been so robust with problems and successes and learning experiences and human experiences that a year is a lifetime at Apple. So this has been ten lifetimes."*

**Sam Walton:** His organization, *Walmart*, became the largest marketer in the world. At the time the dominant stores were large companies like *Sears and Roebuck, Montgomery Ward, Penny's* and *K Mart*. He started a small store in Arkansas in 1945 and built it to be the world's largest seller of merchandize. Sales exceed 450 billion dollars a year. *Walmart* became the largest employer in the world.

Probably his best accomplishment was to build a company with a business plan that survived him and continued to prosper. His story is proof that business is always changing and that opportunities always exist.

*"Capital isn't scarce; vision is."*

*"High expectations are the key to everything."*

*"I have always been driven to buck the system, to innovate, to take things beyond where they've been."*

*"Outstanding leaders go out of their way to boost the self-esteem of their personnel. If people believe in themselves, it's amazing what they can accomplish."*
*"There is only one boss, the customer and he can fire everybody in the company from the chairman on down, simply by spending his money somewhere else."*

**Warren Buffet:** One of the richest persons in the US and a great philanthropist.

*"A public opinion poll is no substitute for thought."*

*"Derivatives are a weapon of mass destruction."*
*"I buy expensive suits; they just look cheap on me."*

*"I do not look for seven-foot bars to jump over; instead I look for a lot of one-foot bars to step over."*

*"If a business does well the market always catches up."*

*"It takes 20 years to build a reputation and five minutes to tear it down. If you think about that you will behave differently."*

**Bill Gates:** Bill Gates was born in 1955 in Seattle. He is recognized as the richest man in America. He remains the largest stockholder of *Microsoft* but resigned as active president and chairman in 2000. He and his wife spend most of their time running the *Bill and Melinda Gates Foundation* which works worldwide to stop diseases.


Quotations from Bill Gates:

*"Be nice to nerds as it is likely you will be working for one someday."*

*"If you can't make it good at least make it look good."*

*"If you think a teacher is tough wait until you get a boss."*

*"Success is a lousy teacher; it makes smart people think they cannot lose."*

## A Closing Thought

I hope my suggestions for good business practices are helpful to ambitious people beginning a career. I only hope my observations are helpful to some.

*"Admit mistakes."*

*"Set an example."*

*"Promote your vision."*

*"Make others feel the importance they deserve.*

Made in the USA
Middletown, DE
06 October 2021